A SHORT GUIDE TO CUSTOMS RISK

SHORT GUIDES TO RISK SERIES

Risk is a far more complex and demanding issue than it was ten years ago. Risk managers may have expertise in the general aspects of risk management and in the specifics that relate directly to their business, but they are much less likely to understand other more specialist risks. Equally, Company Directors may find themselves falling down in their duty to manage risk because they don't have enough knowledge to be able to talk to their risk team in a sensible way.

The short guides to risk are not going to make either of these groups experts in the subject but will give them plenty to get started and in a format and an extent (circa 100 pages) that is readily digested.

Titles in the series will include:

- Climate Risk
- Compliance Risk
- Employee Risk
- Environmental Risk
- Fraud Risk
- Information Risk
- Intellectual Property Risk
- Kidnap and Ransom Risk
- Operational Risk
- Purchasing Risk
- Reputation Risk
- Strategic Risk
- Supply Chain Risk
- Tax Risk
- Terrorism Risk

For further information, visit www.gowerpublishing.com/shortguidestorisk

A Short Guide to Customs Risk

Catherine Truel

GOWER

Published by
Gower Publishing Limited
Wey Court East
Union Road
Farnham
Surrey GU9 7PT
England

Gower Publishing Company
Suite 420
101 Cherry Street
Burlington, VT 05401-4405
USA

www.gowerpublishing.com

British Library Cataloguing in Publication Data
Truel, Catherine.
  A short guide to customs risk. -- (Short guides to business risk)
  1. Customs administration. 2. Risk management. 3. Tariff.
  I. Title II. Series
  658.1'55-dc22

  ISBN: 978-1-4094-0452-1 (pbk)
  ISBN: 978-1-4094-0453-8 (ebk)

Library of Congress Cataloging-in-Publication Data
Truel, Catherine.
  A short guide to customs risk / by Catherine Truel.
    p. cm. -- (Short guides to business risk)
  Includes bibliographical references and index.
  ISBN 978-1-4094-0452-1 (pbk) -- ISBN 978-1-4094-0453-8 (ebook)
  1. Customs administration. 2. Risk. 3. International trade. I. Title.
  HJ6609.T79 2010
  658.1'2--dc22

                                                          2010005765

Printed and bound in Great Britain by
MPG Books Group, UK

Contents

Foreword

As the Secretary General of the World Customs Organization (WCO), I was delighted at being asked to write the foreword to this important and timely book on Customs risk.

ABOUT US

First of all, allow me to introduce briefly the organization that I lead. The WCO is an independent, intergovernmental organization established in 1952 and based in Brussels, Belgium. Uniquely focused on customs matters, the Organization currently has 175 member customs administrations that collectively process approximately 99 per cent of world trade. Our mission is to enhance the effectiveness and efficiency of customs – no easy task given the challenges that befall international trade especially in current times as the world battles to recover from the global economic and financial crisis.

To achieve our mission, we can broadly categorize our activities into five main areas: setting standards for a number of diverse but interlinked customs procedures; promoting international cooperation including information exchange; managing risk; building sustainable capacity including the delivery of quality technical assistance; and enhancing the image of customs as an important state service including its contribution to national economic prosperity and social development.

Indeed, many WCO programmes and projects impact positively on traders' daily cross-border transactions. While I cannot deal with them all, I should nevertheless like to mention a few with the proviso that this list is not exhaustive but merely reflective of the work we are doing to improve the movement of goods and people at frontiers.

RISK MANAGEMENT

Clearly, the array of customs' tasks at the border brings with it an environment fraught with many risks which have to be managed effectively and efficiently to meet the needs of countries and their citizens. The WCO has defined 'risk management' as the systematic application of management procedures and practices that provide customs administrations with the necessary information to address consignments which present a risk. This is essential because the fundamental task of customs is to control the movement of consignments across borders and ensure compliance with national laws and regulations. Risk management can assist customs administrations in allocating resources appropriately so that the impact is fair, effective and efficient.

A selection of instruments, tools and initiatives developed by the WCO provide customs with relevant mechanisms to determine and manage risk. Their efforts are supported by the WCO through vigorous capacity building and technical assistance programmes that are customized to suit regional dynamics and needs.

INTERNATIONAL STANDARDS FOR CUSTOMS AND BUSINESS

The adoption of international standards leads to simplification and harmonization. In this regard, the WCO has developed many standards, ranging from highly technical ones relating to data contained in the WCO Data Model to operational ones set out in the WCO Revised Kyoto Convention on the simplification and harmonization of customs procedures or the trade supply chain security and facilitation standards laid down in the WCO SAFE Framework of Standards to secure and facilitate global trade. The use of these standards in the border environment adds to the effectiveness of customs operations because they provide a predictable trading environment and ensure easier and better compliance from traders.

By promoting an honest and transparent customs environment shored up by our commitment to good governance and integrity, the WCO is also serving the interests of the trade community. But it is equally important for us to interact with business. In this regard a number of trade representatives attend our meetings as observers on a regular basis where they have the opportunity to share their concerns and add to the discussions on customs issues. This important feature gives us an insight into current trade thinking when framing our standards. It goes without saying that the customs-trade partnership is obviously indispensable to the successful implementation WCO instruments and tools.

In many countries, the relationship between customs and trade has evolved from regulator and regulated, to partners. Indeed, it is acknowledged that good partnerships improve customs control and trade facilitation which is essential to economic growth. However, many customs issues have not succeeded in getting to the business world's top management yet some of these issues are critical to success and it is therefore imperative that customs and international trade be better understood by business in general.

TRANSPARENT, PREDICTABLE AND EXPEDITIOUS BORDER PROCEDURES

In today's world, new imperatives such as economic re-expansion, security and environmental protection are bound to bring its own crop of border regulations and controls. These imperatives have added very large and urgent responsibilities to traditional customs practice but they can be offset and made much more acceptable to traders if resulting border controls are focused, rationalized and standardized.

The WCO has been coordinating its efforts with the World Trade Organization (WTO) and UNCTAD to remove some of the remaining barriers to trade by simplifying and harmonizing customs procedures and processes associated with manifold frontier tasks such as the levying and collecting of duties and taxes, enforcing trade policies, and protecting people, animals, plants, intellectual property, cultural heritage and now the environment.

In June 1999, the WCO approved its main blueprint for modern customs procedures; the Revised Kyoto Convention (RKC). Several key governing principles drive the RKC: transparency and predictability of customs actions; standardization and simplification of goods declarations and supporting documents; simplified procedures for authorized persons; maximum use of information technology; the minimum necessary customs controls to ensure compliance with regulations; the use of risk management and audit-based controls; coordinated interventions in cooperation with other border agencies; and a partnership approach with the trade. The RKC promotes trade facilitation and effective controls through its legal provisions that set out simple yet efficient procedures, and contain obligatory rules for its application. Here it may be mentioned that the WTO Trade Facilitation Negotiating Group has recognized the RKC as a valuable source of reference.

Most interesting for our trade partners is the WCO's comparative study of preferential rules of origin which identifies the commonalities between various rules and pinpoints the differences. This work in progress will enable the WCO to propose some best practices which is important in the current trade environment criss-crossed as it is with a plethora of regional trading arrangements.

COMPATIBLE AND CONSISTENT CUSTOMS SECURITY PROGRAMMES

Business is expected to develop a partnership with customs to address security concerns in the post September 11 environment. Many security programmes have been developed around the world to secure global trade and the introduction of incompatible systems worldwide, though they have common aims, raises some issues. Trade needs a single worldwide standard adopted and put into practise. The WCO SAFE Framework of Standards with its 'Authorised Economic Operator (AEO)' concept attempts to do just that but the current disparities between, for example, the US '10+2' requirements and the EU's 'Pre-arrival, Pre-departure (PAPD)' declarations, ostensibly requiring the same data, illustrate the practical difficulties.

While there are slight differences in focus to reflect each country's own priorities, nonetheless, it is important that AEO programmes are compatible and consistent with the standards contained in the SAFE framework. In this regard, the WCO will continue to encourage faster global mutual recognition of AEO programmes while accepting that this may happen slowly but progressively as more and more customs administrations conclude agreements among one another.

A SINGLE WINDOW FOR TRADE

The WCO has been active in the development of the electronic trade single window (SW) concept as a global business model in the arsenal of instruments and tools to facilitate trade. A notorious frustration for traders is data requirements not only from customs but also from other authorities responsible for ports, agriculture, standards, food inspection, trade, environment and immigration. Therefore it is logical for the private sector to be able to submit a single set of data at one time and obtain coordinated goods clearance rather than send different sets of data to various authorities and wait for various replies at different times. This is of course the origin of the single window concept which allows business not only a single submission of data with one designated agency, often customs, but also further promotes collaboration among border agencies for coordinated control.

While there are several SW initiatives taking shape all over the world, there are no clear standards or guidelines governing this area. Customs is increasingly being expected to participate in and take responsibility for the implementation of a SW environment. It is for this reason that the WCO produced an information document for its members entitled 'Single Window: Implications for Customs Administrations' which describes the possible impact that developments around a SW environment have on the future of customs' business. To complement this document, the Organization has also developed its Single Window Data Harmonization Guidelines to provide SW environment developers with tools that can be used to achieve data harmonization and to develop internationally standardized data sets.

In addition, the WCO has established a joint legal task force with the UN Commission on International Trade Law (UNCITRAL) to develop a comprehensive legal guide to the legal implications of implementing a single window. This guide will benefit both governments and the private sector.

HARMONIZED DATA REQUIREMENTS

The WCO Data Model simplifies customs data requirements and provides the basis for integrating data exchange across the whole trade supply chain. This model is a set of carefully combined, mutually supportive and regularly updated standards, designed to meet the procedural needs of customs and other cross-border regulatory agencies concerned with the control of export, import and transit transactions. For business, it also meets the needs of those commercial operators who may need to generate, submit, authenticate and otherwise interchange relevant information for the same purposes.

Many benefits will accrue to those using version 3.0 of the Data Model that was released at the end of 2009. These benefits most notably include the facilitation of trade processes while simultaneously improving enforcement capabilities. There is no longer a need to translate and manipulate data and messages from one system to another, from one document to another, or from many documents into an automated system. Implementation of the Data Model will result in tangible costs savings, improved accuracy and more timely release of goods.

COORDINATED BORDER MANAGEMENT

Enhancing border management and ensuring that it is coordinated is seen as a critical step for the future. There is indeed a need internationally for a radical simplification and harmonization of frontier control systems. Its overall objective being to give trade the operational boon of reliable rapid movement of legitimate consignments through all official controls at all national frontiers. Nothing could be timelier, as the WCO continues to actively engage the G20 and other global policymakers on the urgent need to enlist a wide range of new and improved customs techniques in the all-important task of stimulating and accelerating global trade re-expansion.

This entails cooperation among a variety of government border regulatory agencies. The key challenge is to create an environment based upon trust that allows customs and these agencies to work collaboratively at the border. Within that overall context, the international trade single window using electronic data is an important enabler that provides a technical means for collaboration to be achieved. To facilitate the work of customs at borders, over time the WCO has developed several instruments and tools, and introduced a number of programmes and initiatives, that significantly enhance customs operations. This body of WCO work is constantly being reviewed for its efficacy; it plays a vital role in border management and can contribute enormously to efforts aimed at ensuring even better border management in the future based on coordination, collaboration, cooperation and communication.

Better and smarter border management that is coordinated and that promotes cooperation among all trade stakeholders is the answer to managing borders in the 21st Century. The WCO's instruments, tools and measures already contribute positively to achieving this goal, and its future endeavors will be aimed at enhancing what it has done in the past while at the same time becoming even more innovative. This will ensure a more responsive and strengthened customs community, a more creative and flexible border management, and a better future for all.

GLOBALLY NETWORKED CUSTOMS

I firmly believe that tomorrow's world will be one in which everyone will prosper so I will close by expressing the hope that international trade will become easier to the point that everyone worldwide will be able to enjoy the benefits of the global market equally, using single window technology and electronic systems that enable smooth data transfer to match the flow of goods from country to country; a true globally networked customs with risk management and coordinated border management as its pillars and the business community as its partner.

Developing the 'Globally Networked Customs' concept is already an integral part of the work of the WCO and its members. Its importance to facilitating and securing international trade has already been recognized by the WCO forming as it does one of the ten key building blocks set out in the WCO's Customs in the 21st Century strategic policy which also includes coordinated border management and risk management among others.

IN CONCLUSION

I am quite confident that our approach and our work provide a good basis for managing Customs risk both now and in the future. Further research undertaken by the WCO and its partners on these issues will only enrich our efforts.

This book adds to our arsenal of information, not only influencing our opinions but enabling us to take even better informed decisions. Enjoy reading it, I certainly did.

Yours warmly,

Kunio Mikuriya
Secretary General
World Customs Organization

WORLD CUSTOMS ORGANIZATION

Acknowledgments

During the conception of this book some people have generously shared their expertise and wisdom, others their time, many their encouragement and patience. I am particularly grateful to:

Canada Border Services Agency, Aymeric Chandavoine, Inkyo Cheong, Customs and Excise Department Hong Kong SAR, Julien Duval, Nils Haupt, Korea Customs Service, Otto Kurtz, Paul Man, Kunio Mikuriya, Turloch Mooney, Weihua Ni, Sean Nicoll, Dieter Oppel, Xavier Rochat, Christiane Saunier, Dong Wook Song, Alix Truel, Douglas Tweddle and Wei Xu.

Introduction

Customs authorities worldwide have, in recent years, implemented modernization programs that are fundamentally changing the relationship with the trade community. Perhaps the most powerful aspect of this change is the shift of responsibilities from Customs to traders. In the past, having goods cleared Customs signalled the end of the import or export process. Customs compliance was checked by Customs authorities at the border. Should there be any discrepancy in the documentation, the shipment would stay 'stuck in Customs' for as long as it takes to resolve the discrepancy. But in a world of global supply chains and lean inventories, having goods 'stuck in Customs' for a simple query became unacceptable to the trade community. Customs have been under intense pressure to facilitate and accelerate the clearance of the goods. The trade demanded a separation between the clearance and the release of the goods. Traders argued that goods could be released on arrival while compliance matters could be resolved later. Customs, in many countries, have responded with risk management practices introducing fast and simple clearance at the frontier supported by audit-based controls at the trader's premises. This gives the trade initially a quick release of the goods and subsequently the responsibility to ensure that all compliance requirements are met. Traders must therefore integrate Customs management in their business processes. By moving compliance checks away from the physical border to the company's office, Customs have gained a clear visibility of the physical, documentary and financial supply chain. Global traders have exchanged fast Customs clearance against higher compliance responsibilities.

Customs clearance has evolved from being the end of the Customs transaction to the beginning of the import or export management process. This transfer of responsibilities from Customs to the trade is a source of risk for both the trade and Customs. For traders, these compliance responsibilities cross the company horizontally affecting all departments involved in a transaction. Chapter 1 will look at the risk from the business perspective exploring how modern Customs practices are bringing profound changes to the way global supply chains must be managed. Chapter 2 will turn to Customs authorities to understand how they manage risk and reconcile accelerating and securing border crossings.

By introducing audit-based controls, Customs authorities can follow an entire transaction from quotation to payment. The business must demonstrate a full audit trail from the initial commercial contract through to the payment. For instance, Customs officers could look at the inventory management system to see the imported products being booked into inventory, as well as the financial system to check the value paid to the supplier. During audit-based controls, Customs will use the business records to look at the four basic principles of Customs management: classification, the Customs description of the goods covered in Chapter 3; valuation, the determination of the taxable base, the subject of Chapter 4; or the origin of the goods as explained in Chapter 5.

Customs management is not just about compliance, it can deliver powerful benefits to the business. Customs duties have a direct impact on the cost of the goods sold and the cash flow. Most countries wanting to attract foreign investments, in particular manufacturing, have initiatives to mitigate this impact. They do that with a range of Customs procedures explored in Chapter 6. Some of these procedures will delay the tax point and benefit the cash flow; some will reduce the amount of duty paid while others will remove duties completely. Customs planning is the strategic use of these procedures to generate substantial savings and efficiencies. Customs planning is likely to result in additional compliance requirement, however a company that has acquired the necessary knowledge to manage Customs risk would, at the same time, have prepared the business for Customs planning.

Finally, Customs laws and regulations have not only changed to adapt to the evolution of world trade but also to world events. Since 9/11, global threats and supply chain security has been the focus of new rules adding a new dimension to Customs risk, the subject of Chapter 7.

International trade has its own jargon inherited from history, cultural mix and trends. It is not uncommon to find several words to describe the same process. To reduce the possibilities of confusion and bring harmonization, the World Customs Organization (WCO) has produced a set of terminology and definitions that will be used throughout the chapters. Furthermore, principles and practices are based on the Revised Kyoto Convention (RKO), the agreement governing international Customs management. As most major trading nations are members of the WCO, these principles and practices will be common worldwide. However, their translation into national legislation, availability and day-to-day execution will vary between countries.

3

Customs compliance cannot be confined to a desk at the back of the warehouse anymore. It must be a multidisciplinary exercise. In this new Customs environment, traders must produce, collect, verify and manage a whole trail of documents and data to feed what we can call the compliance chain. All these changes bring new risks and opportunities. Competitive advantage can be gained, lost or simply missed.

(1) Customs Risk and the Business

In its Risk Management Guide, the World Customs Organization (WCO) defines a risk as 'the potential for non-compliance with Customs laws'. From the business perspective non-compliance with Customs laws will translate into three types of risks: regulatory risk arising from laws and regulations, fiscal risk concerned with the collection of duties and taxes, and security risk linked to the integrity of the supply chain.

The negative impact of Customs risk can take many forms:

- *Operational*: Production interruption or production shutdown, delay of a project from its critical path, disruption of the supply chain, loss of sales, increase in inventory costs, late delivery penalties.

- *Financial*: Recalculation of duty and taxes, retroactive duty and taxes assessment, financial penalties, penalties interests, increase in transaction costs, late payment, cash flow and working capital deterioration.

- *Reputation*: Customs risk reported through the accounts, negative press coverage, loss of customers and trading partners, negative impact on credit rating, loss of shareholders and market confidence.

While Customs compliance will brings several benefits:

- *Operational*: Faster clearance, increase in fluidity and speed in the supply chain, decrease inventory levels, improve sourcing strategies.

- *Financial*: Reduced amount of duty paid, ability to sustain profitability, better management of liquidity and cash flow, reduced borrowing, reduced cost of the goods sold.

- *Reputation*: New source of competitive advantage, good reputation, good media reports, good analysts review and good rating agencies analysis.

Customs management is a strategic asset to sustain the business. It must be embedded into the wider business planning because Customs risk has many sources across almost all functions.

SOURCES OF CUSTOMS RISK BY BUSINESS FUNCTIONS

The global supply chain consumes a huge amount of skills, knowledge and expertise to run smoothly. Most events and intermediaries across the global network will have an impact on Customs risk. Internally several departments will directly or indirectly affect the level of risk. The challenge is to link these functions within a multi-disciplinary compliance strategy. The main difficulty is often cultural. Accountants, buyers, sales and logistics are all coming from a different cultural business training and environment. This can create barriers to the cross-departmental collaboration the compliance chain demands.

In practice, Customs and trade compliance can be presented as a series of checkpoints where the global network must comply with demands made by various authorities across several jurisdictions. These checkpoints are conflicting with the principles of global supply chain management because they rely on a different vision. While the global supply chain aims at supporting a constant flow of goods, Customs operate on a transaction per transaction basis. From a Customs perspective, each consignment is treated individually and separately.

STRATEGIC MANAGEMENT

The lack of interest from senior management is the most important and common source of risk. However, despite their best intention, senior executives might not yet have Customs risk on their radar. For instance, the lack of preparation for a change in regulation can disrupt the supply chain. Often, it is during a Customs audit that senior management discovers the business level of exposure to Customs risk. At a time when shareholders are showing an increasing interest in managing global risk, Customs risk needs to be integrated into the business risk management policies and be subject to internal controls.

A business that has decided to buy or sell abroad will be exposed to a new political, economic and cultural environment. A country wanting to attract a particular industry is likely to develop friendly Customs procedures toward that industry. On the other hand, import regulations can make access to a foreign market difficult or even impossible with high duty rates, additional documentary or controls requirements. Customs risk will, in part, depend on a country's trade policy and its import or export requirements. A very demanding set of import regulations specifically designed to keep foreign manufacturers out of the domestic market will increase Customs risk. If the market is due to open in the near future, the objective of the business might be to gain market share and the compliance costs might be a strategic investment. Again, the key is to include Customs and trade risk at the strategic decision level. In some cases, a study of impact to identify Customs risk might uncover some substantial hurdles to an export market. Ultimately, trade policies and Customs regulations will influence the business global strategic decisions. They are at the heart of global sourcing and international sales.

Customs risk can suddenly appear as the result of a merger or an acquisition. Although the due diligence process should pick up any Customs debt, it usually focuses on tax risk and often does not consider Customs risk. The business could still inherit the history of a non-compliance business. This can range from weak internal processes to bad history with Customs authorities. This can affect companies being part of a Customs accreditation program such as the Authorised Economic Operator (AEO) or the US Customs-Trade Partnership Against Terrorism (C-TPAT). Customs risk can also hurt the business ambition of future mergers and acquisitions. Particularly in the US where the Sarbanes-Oxley Act requires, among other things, sound controls for the global supply chain. A business considering a merger or acquisition with a company listed in the US will have to demonstrate not only spotless compliance records but also sound internal procedures and controls.

Corporate restructuring is often a source of Customs risk due to the changes it can bring to the valuation of transactions. Customs and tax authorities have different and conflicting methods to value cross-border transactions.

The choice of trading partners and the management of third party providers will affect the level of Customs risk. The relationship with the Customs agent or broker is critical. Many businesses hold the belief that they do not need to be involved with Customs formalities simply because their logistics provider handles the clearance. This might be right indeed if the logistics provider makes the Customs declaration in its own name. In this case, the logistics provider is the 'declarant' also known as the 'importer of records'. The declarant, in the eyes of the Customs authorities, takes all fiscal and compliance responsibilities. If a formal arrangement is not in place, it is very likely that the importer is the declarant. The high level of risk comes from the fact that the business has outsourced the Customs management function to a logistics provider, an agent or a broker without having any processes and controls to check the compliance level of the transactions made in its name. An extremely dangerous situation. Responsibilities between the business and the service provider must be contractually established. There should be some strong internal controls in place to mitigate this risk.

The business might also be exposed to export control regulations. The export of arms, defence articles and strategic goods is closely monitor by governments and will require a license. Export control applies not only to military products but also to dual-use goods that can be used for both civil and military purposes. Although Customs usually enforce export control, it is often managed by other government agencies.

Customs management is perfectly suited to strategic decision because it operates in a different time horizon from operations. While most functions will be looking at a 12 month time horizon, Customs management looks at 1–5 years ahead preparing for the next change in regulation. In the same way, in case of non-compliance, penalties will often go back several years.

The business level of Customs risk will vary depending on the industry, the product, the region, the countries of origin and destination.

FINANCE

If the finance department is not a great source of Customs risk, of all the business functions, Customs risk affects Finance the most. Mainly because fiscal risk is usually part of the finance director's job description.

The business financial and management accounting system is the tool supporting Customs control-based audits. Customs officers will audit the accounts to check that the information declared at clearance reflects accurately the transaction posted in the accounts. They will, for instance, check that transactions in accounts receivable and accounts payable match orders, invoices, shipping documents and payment. Processes in place to control authorizations for sign-off, credit notes and write-offs will also be of interest. Customs will look closely at inventory movements as well as the inventory value reported in the accounts. The Customs value is not necessary the invoice value. Some costs might be subject to duty and not be mentioned on the invoice. Customs will therefore be interested in cost accounting and cost elements such as treatment of discounts, royalties, financing agreements, commissions and all other service costs that can be associated with a transaction.

However, there is one instance where finance can be at the source of risk, in the case of inter-company transactions. If the business deals with another entity of the same group Customs will want to ensure that the relationship does not affect the value of the goods.

The business also faces the risk of missing an opportunity to reduce the amount of duty paid. This possibility is available only if Finance post Customs duties separately in the accounts. The lack of visibility of how much duty is paid, by product, by origin will not allow the business to identify areas hiding savings opportunities.

PROCUREMENT

The choice of sourcing country will influence Custom risk. For instance, a trade dispute can result in the introduction of trade defence instruments such as quota and anti-dumping duties that will result in higher cost and compliance requirements.

The choice of trading partners will also influence Customs risk. Particularly when procurement is done under the terms of a trade agreement. Trade agreements can require detailed product costing to comply with the rules of origin. This is often complex to set up and the supplier must have the capabilities to implement the agreement requirements. Otherwise, duties will be due at import. Furthermore, security requirements increasingly start at the supplier's factory from traceability to electronic seals. Supplier's relationship management must therefore incorporate Customs compliance. Ideally, suppliers' performance review should include compliance and security processes. Suppliers must also be kept informed of any change or new requirement in the importer's country. For instance, suppliers must now collect additional information to comply with US and EU new Advance Electronic Information Requirements.

Raising a purchase order on a foreign supplier has become the first steps of the import process. Any error at this stage can compromise the compliance chain. The purchase order can be a vehicle for compliance instructions. Some companies use it to mention compliance requirements such as: regular reporting on rules of origin, traceability, or marking requirements.

Misunderstanding International Commerce Terms (Incoterms) such as ExWork, FOB or CIF, is a common source of risk. Although Incoterms specify the point of transfer of risk, cost and ownership from the buyer to the seller, they do not cover Customs legal responsibility. The Customs responsibility will always lie with the declarant/the importer of record.

SALES AND CUSTOMER SERVICES

If the sale is done under the terms of a trade agreement the business will have to comply with the applicable rules of origin. This can be very demanding and evidence shows that some rules of origin can act as hidden protectionism. In this case, despite the trade agreement, the access to the foreign market might be restricted. Consequently, the level of protection in the export market will affect the level of Customs risk.

Optimizing the logistics might not be possible under the terms of a trade agreement as export orders might be subject to direct shipment requirement. Failure to comply with direct shipment instructions will result in the goods being denied reduced rate of duties at import.

For the sales team, the level of Customs risk will vary according to the export market political and economic environment. The sudden introduction of quotas or anti-dumping duties will increase the costs and affect the products competitiveness in the export market. A trade dispute is likely to introduce new requirements and increase the level of Customs risk.

If the business is subject to export control regulations then export orders will require specific attention and possibly a licence. Traders whose activity is affected by export control often use global trade management software to help sales and customer services automate checks required by the regulation. These applications will check products, destination, companies and people relating to the order against the several lists of restrictions. This, both at the time of receiving the order and at the time of export as the lists might have changed between these times.

MANUFACTURING, REPAIR AND SERVICE

Cross-border movements for repair, return, calibration, refill or product recall, use Customs procedures to ensure these transactions are duty free. These procedures are a source of risk, as they will demand strong data management to match the import with the previous export record. The compliance chain will have to track the movement of products sometimes across several borders.

Contracts including an installation abroad will pose a particular risk as products, parts, equipment and tools are likely to cross borders several times. The Customs risk arises from the volume of transactions that will have to be matched with each other to avoid paying duties on the same item several times.

Manufacturing and service often need exceptional consignments such as urgent spare parts, emergency orders, out of hour's shipments or hand carry. These shipments have usually to be arranged in a hurry. Without clear internal processes these transactions pose a risk of non-compliance and expose the business to Customs duties that could have been avoided. Furthermore, repair and service agreements do not always cover the Customs responsibility of returns to suppliers. This can lead to dispute on who pays duty and taxes for in warranty and out of warranty returns.

This department sometimes needs to set up an inventory of spare parts in the export market. This inter-company movement of products can pose a risk resulting from the valuation of the inventory and the value declared at Customs.

Finally, perhaps the most common source of risk from this department is the spare part or the tool thrown in the crate at the last minute before the shipment. The added item is often not mentioned on the invoice and therefore not declared to Customs.

LOGISTICS

The logistics department has a special place in the compliance chain. It is the only department that has both a physical and documentary visibility of the movement of goods. It has therefore a responsibility to ensure that both the physical and documentary flows of goods are compliant. Furthermore, logistics is faced with all Customs risk. Consequently, most decisions from this department can be a source of Customs risk.

In terms of security the physical flow of goods will provide several challenges. Some routes are safer than others. There are many places in a global supply chain where goods can be smuggled into a container. The business needs a security policy and procedures to mitigate this risk and protect the integrity of the supply chain. For instance, a secure warehouse.

Traders monitoring closely lost and stolen cargo can identify specific routes where these events occur. In the same way, Customs know that certain points of the global network are weaker than others. They focus their attention on these locations where consignments have been shipped or trans-shipped. The choice of routing can therefore result in a higher inspection rate whether documentary or physical. In this case, the impact of the risk is the disruption in the supply chain with delay, loss of flexibility and responsiveness. The physical movement of goods could also pose a risk to trade compliance and contravene the direct shipment requirement of a trade agreement.

The document and information flows is the foundation of Customs management, so it has to be accurate and a true representation of the transaction. Weak record keeping from the logistics team is likely to result in non-compliance. There is an unwritten rule in logistics saying that the most competent staff in the warehouse should be at the 'receiving' function. Simply because an error at receiving will be carried across the business. The same rule applies to Customs management because an error at receiving on imported goods will affect the integrity of the import declaration and the compliance record. For instance, a discrepancy between the quantity received and the quantity invoiced will have to be resolved by amending the import declaration.

Furthermore, a lack of accurate recordkeeping can result in a loss of saving opportunity. For instance, when goods are returned to the foreign supplier, the business might be able to reclaim the import duties as long the import and export records can be matched.

But the risk can also be external. Logistics work with intermediaries to move goods across borders. Not all brokers, agents or 3rd party logistics providers are equal. The agent could be a source of risk if its operations are not supported by sound Customs management procedures and controls. Even if carriers, agents and logistics providers have themselves excellent compliance records, a risk can arise from the level of control they have over the services they sub-contract. In many cases, agents and carriers do not have an office in every country. They purchase services from local carriers and agents. The local sub-contractor operations will influence the level of risk. Customs accreditation programs can give an indication of the level of compliance of an agent and its contractors. Ultimately, the Logistics Service Agreement with the carrier should include compliance, security and their relevant key performance indicators.

INFORMATION TECHNOLOGY

The information technology department can be a source of risk as it manages the tools that collect, process, file and report information used for Customs management. For instance, the product file usually keeps data used for the clearance of goods at the part number level such as the tariff codes. It can also contain data required for Customs reporting such as duty rates and restrictions. This information is time sensitive as it is regularly updated and changes need to be implemented within a short window of time.

The IT system must be available to comply with Customs and government reporting deadlines. Any information that is part of the compliance chain must be available on request from Customs authorities.

CUSTOMS RISK AND THE BUSINESS STRUCTURE

Customs management needs a clear line of responsibility and raises the question of the reporting structure. In very large organizations, it will be part of the compliance function. In smaller organizations, it is often found under the finance department. The finance director is responsible for tax compliance, has a keen interest in generating savings and has direct input into the business strategic discussions at board level. Finance is also always represented at board level. Customs management is sometimes placed under logistics. This can create confusion because if logistics deals with Customs clearance, the responsibility for duties and taxes will always remain with the finance department. The fragmentation of Customs responsibilities within the business is a source of risk particularly if the business has multiple divisions, entities and operations in several countries.

Centralizing Customs management allows the business to implement company-wide policies, self-assessments and internal controls to ensure compliance worldwide. However, differences in Customs procedures and practices will demand a differentiated integration. So the global Customs policy will have to be customised to suit local requirements.

Because the source of Customs risk can be found across the organization, Customs management should be independent. Senior management should regularly be briefed on the level of compliance of the business as well as its trading partners by using for instance, Customs metrics.

Customs metrics can include statistical data of inspections, delays, non-compliances, errors, amount of duty paid and share of duty free imports.

The Customs management function can be a global team or just one individual and it is likely to provides services such as:

- Monitor relationship with Customs authorities.

- Identify Customs risk; monitor regulatory changes.

- Develop and maintain Customs policy, processes and procedures.

- Conduct compliance audits internally and of trading partners.

- Deliver training.

- Advise senior management.

MITIGATING RISK: CUSTOMS POLICIES, PROCEDURES AND CONTROLS

Customs regulations and requirements must be implemented systematically. Therefore, a Customs policy containing procedures and processes for administering, managing, measuring and controlling Customs activities will mitigate Customs risk for known and predictable situations.

Self-assessment and internal controls ensure not only that policies and processes are correctly implemented but also that the content is still relevant to the business. Because international trade is an area that is constantly evolving, it is likely that processes will have to be reviewed and adjusted regularly.

The management of Customs risk will ultimately rely on well-trained and knowledgeable staff equipped with accurate data and up to date information. Depending of the level of Customs risk, it might be necessary to train staff from several departments. Customs training is increasingly available from training companies and the World Customs Organization (WCO) has developed online training courses for the private sector covering a wide range of Customs areas.

CUSTOMS INFORMATION, DATA AND DOCUMENT MANAGEMENT

International trade is a paper intensive activity. Very few of the many intermediaries operating along a global supply chain will be in physical contact with the goods. Most decisions are taken based on documents and any discrepancy, delay, loss of products will have to be resolved with only the documents available at the time. International trade is a network of nodes exchanging information and documents with each other. Customs authorities are the only organization positioned at the intersection of all these flows with clear visibility of each trader and each transaction. To get maximum visibility, the business needs a rigorous process to product, check and file accurate and reliable data and documents.

Another force putting a new weight on document management is security. As global infrastructure are becoming more secure, documents can be used to corrupt the supply chain by entering false information not reflecting the actual nature of the shipments. Security principles demand that all documents relating to a cross-border transaction match with each other.

QUICK CHECK

Does the business monitor Customs risk with regular evaluations of Customs processes and internal controls?

Does the business have a reliable procedure to produce, verify and maintain accurate and complete documentation supporting cross-border transactions?

② Customs Risk and Customs Authorities

Globalization has put new demands on Customs authorities. The growth in the volume of trade has put pressure on physical borders. At the same time, the documentation accompanying these shipments has inundated Customs offices with data to be checked and processed. Managing this increase in volume is further complicated by the complexity of trade policies. For instance, the multiplication of trade agreements and trade disputes adds both volume and complexity to the administration of world trade. Meanwhile, the trade community in its quest to build a smooth, continuous global supply chain was demanding faster and simpler Customs clearance. Modernization was indispensable. Global trade was changing and Customs authorities had to adapt their border management to the borderless world.

The role of Customs varies from country to country. However, the core function of a Customs administration covers broadly four main areas: revenue collection; regulatory compliance; trade facilitation; and security. Each area is a source of risk for Customs authorities. Revenue collection was traditionally at the centre of Customs responsibility. However, its importance depends on the share of Customs duties in the national revenue of a country. A study from the World Customs Organization (WCO) shows that in 2005, import duties accounted for 53.3 per cent of Gambia national revenue, 17.31 per cent of India, 4.78 per cent of Brazil, 1.82 per cent of the USA and 0.10 percent of Singapore. The higher the importance of duties in the national budget the stronger the focus on revenue collection. However, in developed countries duties have not disappeared. They have been reduced or removed by trade agreements and Customs procedures. Customs authorities are therefore concentrating their effort on ensuring that goods entering the territory under a procedure or a trade agreement are genuinely entitled to benefit from reduced or nil duty rates. Loss of revenue is always a critical risk area for Customs.

Customs also has the mission to enforce Customs laws as well as a whole range of regulations. Non-compliance with these regulations is a source of risk for Customs authorities.

Another important role for Customs is to facilitate trade. Customs authorities are at the intersection of all trade flows so the efficiency of their operations can enhance the exchange of goods or be a barrier to trade. The World Trade Organization (WTO) has recognized the importance of this role and included trade facilitation in its multilateral negotiations. It is an area of the Doha negotiation round that is rather consensual. In practice, an efficient Customs administration is a competitive advantage for a country. The global infrastructure give traders an extensive choice of routes to move goods between countries and traders will always choose the most efficient path. Businesses will inevitably avoid, whenever possible, a point of entry or exit that will slow their shipments. In fact, it might be cost effective and safer to move a shipment through a longer route to avoid a certain border crossing. There can even be some differences of treatment between Customs offices in the same country. Traders are usually very quick to adapt by changing the routing of their shipments. Customs efficiency is therefore part of the country attractiveness for new businesses and foreign direct investment. Most Customs authorities have therefore embedded trade facilitation principles in their strategic objectives.

Securing the global supply chain is a new challenge for Customs. Since 9/11, some Customs administrations have seen a change in priority toward security. Again, the importance of this role varies between countries with some Customs authorities more centred on security than other. Nevertheless, security is a source of risk for all Customs administrations.

Each Customs administration will balance these roles differently. Some will be focused on revenue collection, others on security. This will be reflected by the place of the organization in the government structure (Widdowson 2007). For instance, if Customs sit under the ministry of finance it is likely to be focused on revenue collection, if like the US it reports to homeland security i's focus will be on security. Consequently, the identification and level of risk will be determined in accordance to the priorities of the Customs administration. Of course, these can change and often do.

Beside their core responsibilities, Customs authorities carry out missions on behalf of other government administrations and agencies. This is where the role of Customs authorities will differ. For instance, they can be asked to:

- Prevent the import of unsafe or dangerous products for departments of health or agriculture.

- Stop movements of endangered species and hazardous waste for environmental agencies.

- Inspect movement of passengers and crews for immigration services.

- Inspect means of transport for the department of transport.

- Collect data from international trade for the department of commerce.

In some cases, the importer or exporter has to obtain an authorization from these agencies or submit the goods for inspection. This is often outside the control of Customs authorities. These agencies can operate in a very efficient manner or add cumbersome procedures to the clearance process. This can slow the movement of goods and still create bottlenecks at the border despite having extremely efficient Customs operations. Although for traders the end result will be the same, the cause of crossborders inefficiencies will not always rest with Customs authorities. Some countries have implemented an Integrated Border Management (IBM) to coordinate the different formalities required at the border.

Beside government agencies, Customs authorities have to manage strategic relationships with a wide range of stakeholders worldwide from private sector organizations to international bodies. They also have to work closely with their foreign colleagues. To operate in this complex international environment and administer global trade efficiently, they need globally harmonized Customs practices. Designing them is the role of the WCO. Created in 1952 the Customs Co-operation Council was renamed in 1994 to the World

Customs Organization. Its role is to develop international agreements and instruments to harmonize and simplify Customs transactions. Perhaps the most influential is the Revised Kyoto Convention.

REVISED KYOTO CONVENTION (RKC)

Considering that inefficient Customs processes can be a barrier to trade, the World Trade Organization asked the WCO to work on harmonizing and simplifying Customs procedures and practices. The result was the Revised Kyoto Convention (RKC). This international agreement introduced standards to simplify and harmonize Customs practices and procedures worldwide.

The original Kyoto Convention, signed in 1973, had already introduced standards for the simplification and harmonization of Customs practices. However, since then, the international trade environment has changed dramatically with growth in volume of trade, reduction of Customs duties, development of information technology. The RKC was adopted at unanimity in 1999 and entered into force in February 2006.

The RKC recognizes several principles:

- The importance of predictability and transparency in Customs procedures and practices.

- The importance of providing the trade with all necessary information regarding Customs such as law, regulation, guidelines, advices, procedures.

- The adoption of modern technology, risk management and audit control.

- An easy accessible process for administrative and judicial review.

The RKC has three parts: the body, the general annex and specific annexes. The body contains the main provisions. The general annex contains ten chapters with basic principles covering: the clearance of goods, duties and taxes, guarantees, controls, information technology, relationship with third parties, dissemination of information, decision and appeal. The specific annexes contain standards and practices on individual Customs procedures. Countries joining have to accept the body and the general annex but the specific annexes are not mandatory. However, a country accepting a specific annex or chapter will be bound by all standards contained in them. The RKC also includes implementation guidelines detailing methods, examples and best practices. The convention provides useful definitions to harmonized Customs terminology so the same procedure is not called differently across the planet. In addition, it defines a standard for statistics.

As other agreements and conventions designed by the WCO, the RKC offers a high degree of uniformity. At the same time, the specific annexes, that can be adopted in part or in full offers a degree of customization. This flexibility can be criticised for reducing uniformity but it allows each country to tailor the RKC to its own specific environment. It also allows gradual modification of current Customs practices in the case of developing countries for instance. To implement the RKC, countries signatories usually have to modify their national legislation introducing changes that not only affect Customs authorities but also traders and other government agencies.

In many countries, the RKC has been the driver behind Customs modernization programs and the introduction of risk management. The RKC represents a profound paradigm shift for Customs authorities worldwide and completely changes the way Customs operate.

THE POWER OF COMPUTERIZATION

Customs used to receive paper invoices from manufacturers, printed transport documents from carriers, manual Customs declaration from Customs brokers. Because Customs clearance is done on a transaction per transaction basis, every consignment is cleared through Customs separately. Consequently, the increase of volume of trade affects directly Customs operations. In addition, the introduction of risk management processes demand that the information collected be analysed and compared. Treating such a volume of data required computerization.

In many countries, Customs collect information electronically. Traders, brokers, agent, carriers, port facilities operators directly enter data into Customs computer system using Direct Trader Input (DTI). To manage these data Customs use a wide range of IT solutions, some more sophisticated than others. As a result of the RKC, many Customs authorities have been updating their computer system. Some of them are just starting to move away from paper-based declarations, others are implementing cutting edge solutions. Usually a Customs computer system can:

- Process Customs declarations and clear goods.

- Allow initial clearance with minimum information.

- Assess, collect, defer revenue.

- Control tariff and description of products.

- Control the value of goods.

- Control movements of cargo at import, export or in transit.

- Manage traders accounts.

- Analyse data to assess the level of risk.

- Support control-based audits.

- Produce statistics, strategic reporting.

Nevertheless, often data has to be submitted not just to Customs but also to different government agencies. These various administrations require different content often in a different format. To avoid the multiplication of data content and format requirement within one country, the WCO recommend the adoption one single point of collection for all information required by all agencies in the country. The 'Single Window' concept allows traders to enter all information, once, at the time of the Customs declaration. Data are then electronically transferred to the relevant government departments. The single window is pushing further the harmonization of data, the elimination of duplication but requires co-ordination between agencies.

For instance, in 2004, Korean Customs Service (KCS) established an internet-based Customs portal giving traders access to 162 administrative services such as submission of import declarations, application for duty drawback. In 2008, KCS developed the portal into a Single Window connecting 14 different government agencies generating savings of more than US $3.5 billions.

Some countries such as Singapore have gone further into integration. The TradeNet system links Customs application to the entire trade community such as banks.

But the variety of IT solutions implemented worldwide has resulted in different format and content requirements between countries. This is a problem for global traders that need to use different data sets for their global operations. It is also a problem for Customs as it complicates the exchange of information between Customs authorities. To ensure harmonization, the WCO has developed the Customs Data Model. This standard covers the content and format of Customs data requirements and communication exchange between Customs and the trade.

The Data Model was a project of the G7 countries that recognized, in 1996, the need to standardize Customs data requirements. The Data Model has been managed by the WCO since 2002 and provides an international standard for data sets and electronic messages. It defines the maximum set of data for all import and export formalities. The Data Model is regularly reviewed to extend its area of influence and integrate data requirements from other government bodies.

Automation and computerization have changed the way goods are cleared. Traders can use pre-arrival Customs processing facility to submit clearance data to Customs in advance of the arrival of the goods. Customs system will automatically process the data and run the risk management checks. Following the processing of the data the goods are released to the trader.

The electronic clearance of cargo can make border crossing an intangible experience for the trader. Customs clearance can be immediate and in many cases can happen before goods physically arrive at the border.

A CUSTOMS VIEW OF RISK MANAGEMENT

Risk management is defined by the WCO risk management guide as: 'the systematic application of management procedures and practices which provide Customs with the necessary information to address movements or consignments which present a risk'.

Like the trade, Customs authorities are faced with three main risks: compliance, fiscal and security. Controls for these risks used to take place at the border. The introduction of risk management replaced controls at the border with automated analysis.

PROFILING AND TARGETING

Customs authorities collect every day a vast amount of information from a wide variety of sources such as: shipping manifest, goods declarations, audits, results from risk analysis or data from other Customs agencies. By using qualitative and quantitative analytical tools, Customs gain visibility into trading practices of a country, a specific industry or a particular trader. This will help identify emerging practices by industry, unusual routes by product or a change in pattern by a trader. It can also show combinations that could be a source of risk.

Based on this information, Customs can build risk profiles against which consignments will be checked. The WCO Risk Management Guide defines a risk profile as a 'predetermined combination or risk indicators, based on information which has been gathered, analysed and categorized'.

Risk profiles are the result of risk assessment and include several indicators such as:

- Trader's compliance records.

- The nature and value of the goods, for instance, goods subject to high duty rates, restriction and quotas.

- The nature of the transaction.

- Certain industries known for their compliance problems.

- Certain regulations or Customs procedures that usually pose compliance issues.

- The country of origin and destination.

- The place of loading, port of trans-shipment, free trade zones.

- The routing and the mode of transport.

- The operators involved such as manufacturers, logistics providers and ports.

- Financial consequence of non-compliance.

Risk profiling focuses the activity on risk areas while still including spot checks. The risk management system checks the data against the risk profiles and determines the appropriate level of attention for shipments by directing them to one of the clearance channel:

- The green channel releases goods immediately after the payment or deferment of duty and taxes.

- The blue channel releases goods immediately and refer the transaction to an audit-based control.

- The orange channel indicates documentary inspection.

- The red channel sends the shipment for documentary and physical inspection for part or whole of the consignment.

Goods directed to the orange channel can either progress to the green channel if all is in order and be released to the trader; or be forwarded to the blue or red channel for additional examination. Goods sent to the red channel will be inspected using equipments such as X-ray or scanners as under the RKC, Customs authorities must prefer non-intrusive method of inspection. Customs also use the orange and red channels to check the reliability of their risk management system. They can, for instance, redirect a consignment from the green channel to the orange or red channel to ensure that their risk management system has not missed anything.

In case of a trader recurring non-compliance, Customs can set up a risk profile that will direct all import from this particular trader to the red channel. In the same way, a risk profile can be applied to a country, supplier, carrier, agent or a combination of all. Risk profiles are also regularly modified.

The release of the goods is not necessarily the end of the Customs process. During an audit-based control, Customs will look at all transactions in more details. The physical presence of the goods is not required to spot a non-compliance; documents and accounting transactions are enough. Audit-based controls can therefore uncover non-compliance several years after the goods have been used.

AUDIT-BASED CONTROLS

The RKC defines audit-based control as: 'measures by which Customs satisfy themselves as to the accuracy and authenticity of declaration through the examination of the relevant books, records, business systems and commercial data held by persons concerned'.

The decision to conduct an audit can be driven by a risk profile. It can result from a particular focus on an industry. It can also be part of an annual audit program. The audit can be transaction-based and look at one or several individual transactions. It can be company-based and look at the level of compliance of the whole business. Customs can during a transaction-based audit notice a series of non-compliances and change the focus to a company-based audit. The period under scrutiny can vary. Customs can look at current transactions or look back for several years.

PROSECUTIONS AND SANCTIONS

The best approach to Customs and trade compliance is voluntary compliance. This is easier and cheaper for Customs and for businesses. However, when necessary, Customs have several tools to deal with non-compliance. The sanctions will be dependent on the country, the trader's Customs processes, past records, the nature of the non-compliance and its impact on revenue or security.

The RKC specifies that genuine errors should not be punished by heavy penalties. A typical genuine error can be a typing mistake. It can also be goods that have been over-shipped, showing five items on the invoice but having six articles in the box. Once the trader has noticed the error, it can follow a formal process to amend the import declaration and therefore correct the error. There can also be errors due to the lack of knowledge from a new trader. This is more serious as the business should have knowledgeable staff dealing with Customs matters. At the lower end of the sanction scale, Customs can usually provide some technical assistance and advice. However, if Customs declarations are never checked and the business lacks reliable procedures and controls then 'informed compliance' will not be appropriate. Customs can conclude that the business has ignored its responsibility and shown a lack of care. At this point, depending on the country, Customs can issue a formal warning, raise penalties, charge interest, remove authorizations and certifications. They can also modify the business risk profile so all imports are systematically directed to the red channel.

In many countries, traders have not kept up to date with the modernization of Customs and are surprised by the increase in audit-based controls. Customs scrutiny is not limited to domestic operations. Increasingly, Customs collaborate with their foreign colleagues to conduct global Customs audits across all international divisions of the business. Consistent compliance becomes critical. An importer with a past history of non-compliance will pose a higher level of risk and therefore demand more attention.

QUICK CHECK

Can the business demonstrate that it does not pose a compliance, fiscal or security risk to the Customs authority?

Does the business have an individual with sufficient knowledge of Customs management to ensure requirements are met?

(**3**) Classification

Because global trade operates through many languages, it is critical to be able to describe the same product in the same way across the world. Therefore the trade community needs a universal system to identify every product in every language along the global supply chain. This is the role of the Harmonized Commodity Description and Coding System developed by the World Customs Organization (WCO) and introduced in 1988. Usually called the Harmonized System (HS), it is part of the International Convention on the Harmonized Commodity Description and Coding System, and replaces the Convention on Nomenclature for the Classification of Goods in Customs Tariff of 1950. Classification is the process to select and assign a six digit HS code for the precise description of a product to the Customs authorities. The HS code is also known as: commodity code, tariff number, tariff code.

The HS describes products with a common language that can cross languages and culture. For example: a pen can be a ball pen, a fountain pen, a felt-tipped pen. Differentiating between these pens becomes important if these types of pen are subject to different duty rates. A specific description is also very useful for trade statistics. For instance, an exporter of fountain pens might want to know the size of an export market for its own products and not for all types of pen.

Countries members of the WTO must use the HS for statistical and Customs tariff nomenclature. The Customs tariff also known as tariff schedule being the document listing all HS codes and containing among other things Customs duty rates. To clarify the terminology, the WCO defines Customs duties as 'the duties laid down in the Customs tariff to which goods are liable on entering or leaving the Customs territory'. The Customs territory is defined as 'the territory in which the Customs law of a Contracting Party applies'. This element is important, as the Customs territory is often different from the national territory. In the US, for instance, the Customs territory covers: the States, the District of Columbia and Puerto Rico.

The vast majority of goods traded globally are identified using the HS. The Customs tariff nomenclature serves a multitude of purposes:

- Determine duty rate.

- Identify restrictions and prohibitions.

- Monitor trade policies and rules of origin.

- Implement quotas.

- Provide accurate and comparable data for trade negotiation and trade disputes.

- Build WTO schedules.

- Standardize the collection, analysis and comparison of international trade statistics.

- Match import and export trade statistics.

- Calculate freight tariff and international transport statistics.

- Support economic research.

CLASSIFICATION AS A SOURCE OF RISK

Classification is a one of the four basic principles of Customs management. It applies to all products crossing borders: finished goods, components, spare parts, engineer tools, commercial leaflets, exhibition materials. A wrong classification is a misrepresentation of the product. It can be a genuine error, a wrong interpretation of a definition or an intention to hide the true nature of the goods.

The HS nomenclature comprises:

- 21 sections.

- 97 chapters at 2 digit level.

- 2 final chapters 98 and 99 for national use.

- 1,241 headings (4 digit level).

- 5,000 approx. subheadings (6 digit level).

- 200,000 numerical codes of products.

- 6 general rules for the interpretation. These are the classification rules that must be applied to determine the code of a product.

- Section, chapter and heading notes clarifying definitions by giving details of products included and excluded from the definitions.

- The possibility to include further subdivisions after the subheading for national use. For instance, the EU and the US HS codes have 10 digits.

However, like always with Customs management, slight differences of names will appear between countries. In the EU, the Customs tariff is called the 'Combined Nomenclature (CN) of the European Community.' In the US, it is known as the 'Harmonized Tariff Schedule of the United States' (HTSUS) and is managed by the US International Trade Commission. However, the US also use export codes called 'Schedule B' and managed by the US Census Bureau. Both have ten digits and are identical up to the six digit of the subheading.

Assigning an HS Code to a product is the result of a process. It is systematic with strict rules. It is therefore possible internally to design a procedure to cover classification. The HS is designed in a logical structure with a progression according to the degree of sophistication of a product. Classification must therefore be carried out following the hierarchical structure of the HS. Goods must first be classified within a section, chapter, then within a heading and only then within a subheading. A product has only one HS code. For instance, a manufacturer of musical instrument having to ship a piano will look at:

Section XVIII – optical, photographic, cinematographic, measuring, checking, precision, medical or surgical instruments and apparatus; clocks and watches; musical instruments; parts and accessories thereof:

Chapter 92 – Musical instruments; part and accessories of such articles.

9201 Pianos, including automatic pianos; harpsichords and other keyboard stringed instruments.

9201 10 Upright pianos.

9201 20 Grand pianos.

9202 90 Other.

In practice, classification is done using a widge range of information:

- The Customs tariff: sections, chapters and subheading notes.

- General rules of interpretation.

- Explanatory notes. These are official interpretations and guidance, however, not legally binding.

- *HS Compendium of Classification Opinions*. Published by the WCO, it contains decisions issued by the WCO Harmonized System committee.

- Rulings previously issued by Customs authorities for similar products. In many countries these are available online for traders to consult.

- Product brochures, catalogues, technical specifications.

- In addition, internally, engineering, technical research department will be useful to understand the intrinsic quality of a product while the sales force will give an insight on the use of a product. The variation in explanations could be the indication of a complicated classification process.

Customs classification can be a source of risk for several reasons:

- *The nature of the products*: high-tech or new products where the HS does not yet have an appropriate position describing the product. This is the case, for instance, for some new environmental products.

- *The function of the product*: sometimes a product can have several functions and it might be difficult to identify the intrinsic and defining function. For instance, a computer monitor is classified under subheading 8471 60 under the description of a computer 'input and output unit'. A video monitor is classified 8528 21. What about a computer monitor that receives video signal from other equipments such as a DVD player and game console? It is a computer monitor and a video monitor so where should it be classified? In 2004, in the EU, a company imported widescreen LCD monitors. These monitors can be connected to a computer as well as other equipments. The importer classified the goods as computer monitors. In countries signatories of the Ministerial Declaration on

Trade in Information Technology Product (1996), computer monitors are subject to zero percent duty.. The importer therefore expected the product to be imported into the EU duty free. However, the Dutch Customs authorities disagreed with the classification. They considered that since the monitor could also be used with DVD players and game consoles it had to be classified as a video monitor and was therefore subject to the 14 percent duty rate. This resulted in a long dispute, the Kamino Case, resolved in 2009 when the European Court of Justice that decided that these LCD monitors should be classified as computer monitors (zero per cent duty).

- *The volume of products*: a large bill of material that can be imported separately, for instance, sub assemblies, spare parts or accessories will have to be classified independently. Spare parts and accessories are not classified in the same way and there often is a substantial difference between rates of duty.

- *The tariff position*: it is possible that Customs authorities in different countries have allocated different tariff positions for the same product. For instance, fountain pens are found in different places in the EU, Japanese and Australian tariff.

Fountain pens are classified as:

Section XX Miscellaneous manufactured articles.

Chapter 96 Miscellaneous manufactured articles.

Heading 9608 Ballpoint pens; felt-tipped and other porous-tipped pens and markers; fountain pens, stylograph pens and other pens; duplicating stylos; propelling or sliding pencils; penholders, pencilholders and similar holders; parts (including caps and clips) of the foregoing articles, other than those of heading 9609.

But at the subheading differences appears:

EU tariff:

9608 10   Ballpoint pens.

9608 20   Felt-tipped and other porous-tipped pens and markers.

9608 31   *Fountain pens*, stylograph pens and other pens including Indian ink drawing pens.

Japan tariff:

9608 10   Ball point pens.

9608 20   Felt tipped and other porous-tipped pens and markers including *Fountain pens*, stylograph pens and other pens.

9608 31   Indian ink-drawing pens.

9608 39   Other.

Australia tariff

9608 10   Ballpoint pens.

9608 20   Felt-tipped and other porous-tipped pens and markers.

9608 3   *Fountain pens*, stylograph pens and other pens.

9608 31 00   Indian ink drawing pens.

A manufacturer of fountain pens trading in the EU, Japan and Australia will be confronted with three different HS codes. In this case, it will be impossible to centralize the classification of this product.

A wrong classification represents a risk for Customs and for the business. For Customs, it is potentially a loss of revenue. For the business, it is a source of non-compliance, it is also the possibility of paying the wrong amount of duty or paying duty that is not due. There is also the risk of importing a product that, if classified under the correct code, would be subject to restrictions or even prohibition.

Wrong classification can happen for various reasons:

- Lack of knowledge of the classification process.

- Lack of understanding of the product.

- Lack of internal communication. For instance, within the same organization one factory can use a HS code while another uses a different one.

- Lack of external communication. In the case where the company's HS codes are not provided to business partners such as the agents or carriers. HS codes declared at Customs can therefore vary depending on the agent completing the Customs declaration. For instance, the 3rd party logistics provider might classify the product as an accessory while the previous declaration handled by an express carrier classified the goods as spare parts.

- Lack of internal assessments and controls.

- The intent to hide the true nature of the goods.

There are several reasons for trying to hide the nature of the goods. The most common is paying as little Customs duty as possible. The scenarios are well known by Customs. For instance, the classification of high value products is moved to an HS code with a lower duty rate. For this reason, the person responsible for classification should have the support of the senior management to avoid being pressurized into selecting an HS code with a lower rate. In some organizations, the person classifying goods is independent to ensure the integrity of the classification process. Ultimately, Customs risk management system will pick up classification errors, genuine or intentional. From historic data, they'll know if mis-classification is particularly common on certain products, industries, countries or traders. They will increase scrutiny on these transactions by, for instance, creating a risk profile.

To satisfy an audit-based control, each classification exercise should produce a file supporting the decision for the selection of the HS code including the classification methodology, commercial or technical brochures. Not being able to fully justify the classification and provide supporting evidence of the decision is a risk.

CLASSIFICATION AS A SOURCE OF OPPORTUNITY

Accurate classification gives visibility of the various treatments of a product worldwide. With the HS code a business can find the various duty rates, restrictions and prohibition for its product. If the business has competitors in different countries, it can find whether a trade agreement reduces duty rates in a certain export markets for its own operation, for competitors or both. In that sense, an accurate HS code provides predictability.

Many Customs authorities have classification specialists providing advice and guidance on the classification process. Customs also issue binding rulings on the classification of a product. Advance ruling is a formal process to request, from Customs, a legally biding decision. This allows a business to be confident that its product classification is compliant.

Accurate classification increases the chances of using successfully some Customs procedures for duty reduction. Often classification errors prevent a business from obtaining a refund of Customs duty. This is the case when the business cannot prove that the same product has been imported and subsequently exported because the HS code used at import is different from the HS code used at export.

HS codes provide harmonization not just for world trade but also at the business level. Several business functions use HS codes: The procurement department to check duty rates for their purchases, the sales force to consider the impact of duty on export markets, the IT team to update the product file with new updates. HS codes should also be distributed to external partners. In the first instance, the agent that will clear goods, but also to suppliers and customers. Harmonization permitting, it should also be used across international divisions.

The HS code can help decide at which stage of the manufacturing process semi-finished products should be moved between manufacturing or distribution centres. A product will have a different HS code at each manufacturing stage, from components, sub-assembly and assembly to finished product. The duty rates attached to these codes could be different for each stage. Using logistics postponement techniques to customize or assemble the product close to the customer market might be further efficient if matched with a reduced import duty rate.

Working on the classification of a product in collaboration with the research and design team can result in a product specifically conceived to attract a low duty rate. Providing of course that Customs authorities are satisfied with the classification. The objective of 'Tariff engineering' is to insert into the design of a product the intrinsic qualities necessary for a product to be qualified under a certain code instead of another. Sometimes a product that has been the subject of small modifications can change classification position. The danger is that products can be reclassified quite easily by government, as a result of a dispute or an update of the HS by the WCO.

Classification is not static, it evolves constantly. Changes to the HS come from countries regularly reclassifying products, national Customs authorities issuing classification rulings, national courts of justice ruling on classification issues and trade lobbying for new codes. These changes are centralized at the WCO Harmonized System committee responsible for the management of the HS. The WCO committee handles disputes on the interpretation of certain descriptions. It produces clarification opinion and decision. The objective is to ensure that there is only one possible interpretation of a product classification and description.

Because the HS system is extensively used and is a foundation of the trading system, changes and amendments impact on many areas of international trade. The Harmonized System Committee of the WCO produces amendments every 5–6 years. Amendments are necessary to:

● Adapt HS codes and descriptions to new products, new technology.

● Respond to demand from the trade.

● Include opinions and decisions issued from the HS committee on semantic disputes and differences of interpretation.

Any exercise of reclassification, amendment of HS code will have a series of impact on the business. For instance, two codes with different duty rates might be merged into one. Or a code might have to be divided to accommodate a new product. This can affect the business with an increase or decrease of duty rates.

The latest WCO HS amendments were implemented in 2007. HS2007 is the current version of the Harmonized System. The WCO council has adopted the next set of amendments in June 2009. WCO members have 6 months to object to an amendment. All amendments accepted will enter into force on 1 January 2012. HS2012 is the fifth amendment of the HS and contains 221 sets of amendments. The main changes include new additions covering environmental products. In addition, 40 subheadings with low usage will be deleted. New subheadings will be added to name separately products that were previously not clearly identified.. For instance, the HS2012 contain the following amendment:

CHAPTER 96.

Delete Subheadings 9608.3 to 9608.39 and substitute: '9608.30 – Fountain pens, stylograph pens and other pens'.

Consequently, as a result of HS2012, fountain pens will be individually identified.

The doubt about the fountain pen classification will be removed bringing worldwide harmonization. Fountain pen manufacturers will now have to follow this development to check how it will influence the duty rate.

QUICK CHECK

Can the business demonstrate that all products crossing borders have been classified with the correct HS code in accordance with the regulation?

Has the business obtained a classification ruling for the Customs authorities?

(4) Valuation

The value of a product is formed by several cost elements such as material, processing, delivery and profit. In addition the value can be expressed in several ways, for instance, in terms of cost or price. It would be extremely inefficient if each country developed its own calculation method to value the goods arriving at its border. International trade therefore uses a standard valuation methodology. Valuation, one of the four basic principles of Customs management, is the process used to calculate the value of the goods for Customs purposes. This value is the taxable base upon which duties and taxes will be assessed.

In 1947, the General Agreement on Tariffs and Trade (GATT) negotiations concluded that the Customs value should not be arbitrary or fictitious. Since then, a series of agreements has formed what are today the valuation rules.

The valuation rules are based on the 'Agreement on the Implementation of Article VII of the General Agreement on Tariffs and Trade (GATT) 1994'. Called the WTO Customs Valuation Agreement (CVA), it is a set of rules that must be used to determine the value of the goods for Customs clearance. Since the WTO Uruguay Round (1994), the CVA is mandatory for WTO members. Valuation rules are used to:

- Determine and collect revenue.

- Produce trade statistics.

- Implement and monitor trade agreements.

- Monitor quantitative restrictions.

VALUATION AS A SOURCE OF RISK

From Customs perspective the risk is the loss of revenue and for traders it is non-compliance, heavy penalties and missed opportunity of generating savings.

Valuation is a particularly important area for Customs because a wrong valuation will usually affect revenue even if the goods imported are duty free. This is because Customs, at import, often collect several other taxes beside duties for instance Value Added Tax. The taxable base is therefore critical to revenue collection and explains the intense scrutiny that traders might be experiencing in that area.

Customs therefore want to determine whether the value declared is the true value. Hiding the true value of the goods is usually done through invoicing as it is quite easy to falsify an invoice. Methods are well known such as:

- *Under invoicing*: having one invoice for the country of export and one for the country of import. Or having a shipping invoice to accompany the goods and another invoice for payment. During an audit-based control Customs will look at the commercial and accounting system to check that the value declared at import not only matches with the invoice posted in the account, but also with the relevant payment.

- *Over-invoicing*: it is used to move funds out of a country, for instance, when there are restrictions on foreign currencies. It also can be used by a group wanting to move profit from a high tax to a low tax country.

- *Small consignements*: the objective is to have the value of the goods remain under a certain threshold to avoid certain requirements, restrictions or taxes.

Customs risk management system will detect valuation errors, genuine or intentional. Customs valuation databases collect the value of each HS code at import and export allowing comparison and analysis by product, industry and country of origin or trader. Customs authorities also collect information on world market prices and their evolution on almost every product. In addition, they share information with other Customs authorities. Ultimately, they can create a risk profile to capture non-compliance.

The Customs value is not necessarily identical to the invoice value. The determination of this value follows valuation principles. The Custom Valuation Agreement defines the Customs value as 'the transaction value of the imported goods, which is the price actually paid or payable for the goods when sold for export to the country of importation'.

The Customs value is determined on a transaction per transaction basis by applying one of the six methods of valuation. However, the selection of the valuation method must follow a hierarchical order starting with method 1: the transaction value. Only if the transaction value cannot be applied then the importer can consider using method two and so on. The exception is with method 5 and 6 where the importer can request to use any of them.

The vast majority of goods are clearing Customs under method 1.

METHOD 1 – THE TRANSACTION VALUE

According to the Value Agreement: 'The transaction value of the imported goods is the price actually paid of payable for the goods when sold for export to the country of importation' plus or minus certain adjustments.

The price 'actually paid or payable' means all payments related to the imported goods. These payments can, for instance, be made before or after the time of import. They might be invoiced with the goods or separately. If these payments are not included in the commercial invoice then the value declared at Customs will have to be adjusted to obtain the transaction value. Article 8 of the Customs Valuation Agreement describes costs to add to the invoice value of the imported goods:

1. Costs incurred by the buyer but not included in the price for the goods:

    - Selling commissions and brokerage.
    - Cost of containers which are treated as being one purposes with the goods.
    - Cost of packing for labour or materials.

2. Part of the value of goods or services supplied directly or indirectly to the buyer free of charge or at reduced costs:

- Materials, components, parts and similar items incorporated in the imported goods.
- Tools, dies, moulds and similar items used in the production of the imported goods.
- Materials consumed in the production of the imported goods.
- Engineering, development, artwork, design work, and plans and sketches undertaken elsewhere than in the country of importation and necessary for the production of the imported goods.

3. Royalties and license fees related to the goods that the buyer must pay as a condition of the sale (payment for patents, trademarks and copyrights).

The value of any part of the proceeds of any subsequent resale, disposal or use of the imported goods that accrues directly or indirectly to the seller.

The value of some of these cost elements is likely to cover an entire production run that will be imported in several shipments over a period of time. There will therefore be a need to allocate these costs to the imported products. Businesses running cost-based accounting will be able to use their cost allocation process to attribute costs to a specific product. With this costing information the value to be added to the invoice price can be divided over several imports. Alternatively, the value might simply be added to the first shipment. This decision will have cash flow implications.

Because, the price actually paid or payable applies to the imported goods, any payment not related to the imported goods is not part of the Customs value. Even if it is included in the invoice as long as it is individually identified.

Customs valuation is therefore a process of 'unbundling' the costs to determine what is dutiable and what is not. This will allow a business to remove certain costs included in the price but not liable to duty and therefore decrease the taxable base.

In addition, each country can choose to include or exclude in whole or in part from the Customs value:

- The cost of transport to the port of importation.

- Loading, unloading and handling charges relating to the transport of the imported good to the place of importation.

- The cost of insurance.

For instance, Article 55 of the Customs Law of the People's Republic of China specifies that: 'The Customs valuation of import goods shall include the value of the goods, cost of transport, charges associated with transport of the goods and cost of insurance occurred before the goods are unloaded at the entering point of the territory of the People's Republic of China'. This is similar to EU valuation while in the US valuation does not include any transport or insurance cost.

If the buyer and seller are related, such as companies being part of the same group, the transaction value can still be used based on the arm's length principle. Defined by the Organisation for Economic Co-operation and Development (OECD), this principle states 'transactions should be valued as if they had been carried out between unrelated parties, each acting in his own best interest'. In effect, the relationship must not influence the price.

Valuation is done using a wide range of information:

- Valuation regulation.

- Customs rulings.

- Decisions and opinions from the WCO technical committee on Customs valuation.

- Purchase orders and contracts.

- Invoices, purchase ledger, account payable, cost accounting systems.

Reliable supporting documentation is crucial to determine and demonstrate accurate valuation. To satisfy an audit-based control, like for classification, the valuation exercise should produce a file with costing evidence justifying costs that have been included or excluded. Not being able to fully justify the valuation is a source of risk.

Since most of the goods traded globally clear Customs using method 1, other methods covered by the valuation agreement are not as common:

- Method 2 'Transaction value of Identical goods sold for export to the same country of import and exported at or about the same time'.

- Method 3 'Transaction value of Similar goods sold for export to the same country of import and exported at or about the same time'.

- Method 4 'Deductive value which is the Unit price at which the imported goods or identical or similar are sold in the greatest aggregate quantity to an unrelated party at or at about the time of the importation with some adjustment'.

- Method 5 'The computed value which is the sum of the cost or value of material and fabrication or other processing employed in producing the imported goods. Including an amount of profit and general expenses equal to that usually reflected in sales of goods of the same class or kind as the goods being valued'.

- Method 6 – Fallback value. 'The value is calculated using reasonable means consistent with the principles and general provisions of the agreement and on the basis of data available in the country of importation'.

The Valuation Agreement is governed by the WTO committee on Customs Valuation and maintained the WCO Technical Committee on Customs Valuation. Like for classification, the WCO committee looks at technical problems and issue advisory opinions and commentaries. WCO decisions have a profound impact on the way trader value goods at Customs. For instance, in 2007, the committee Commentary 22.1 'Meaning of the Expression Sold for Export to the Country of Importation in a Series of Sales' might indicate the end of the 'first sale' rule. This would force many multinational corporations to redesign their global supply chain.

The 'first sale' rule allows, under certain conditions, importers to value goods sold through a chain of intermediaries by using the price of the first sale in the chain as the Customs value. For instance, in the case of a manufacturer in China selling the goods to a middleman in Hong Kong who in turn sells the good to a US trader. The Customs value at import in the US would normally be the price between the middleman and the US trader. However, under certain circumstances, the Customs value can be the 'first sale' price from the manufacturer in China. This can generate substantial savings. First sale is based on the transaction value and is available in the US, the EU and Japan. Australia and Canada have abolished the first sales rule.

In the commentary, the committee suggests that the price should be the last sale before import and not the first sale.

This extremely influential commentary has created intense debate among the international trade community. In many large groups, the first sale rule has been the foundation on which the entire global supply has been designed. Removing this rule will result in companies having to redesign their Customs planning in order to limit the cost increase that would result from such a decision. This is likely to impact on the business sourcing strategy.

VALUATION CONTROL

Valuation is usually checked during audit-based control when Customs have access to the business accounts. As a consequence, valuation disputes don't have to stop the flow of goods. Provision of Article 13 of the WTO Customs Valuation Agreement states that when the value is under dispute, the trader should be able to withdraw the goods against guarantee such as deposit or bond. The Valuation Agreement specify that valuation controls have to be based on Generally Accepted Accounting Principles (GAAP) which are countries accounting rules and standards. Customs will therefore conduct a valuation audit using information produced by and available in the accounting and financial system.

Developing countries that do not have the manpower or tools to carry out controls at import use Pre-Shipments Inspections. The import control checks are therefore done in the country of export. A Pre-Shipment Inspection company checks the value of the goods, the quantity and the classification to issue a certificate. The main objective is to identify under-invoicing and support revenue collection.

Although valuation rules worldwide are based on the valuation agreement, they are often interpreted and implemented differently across the world. This can be the source of uncertainties and risk for companies operating in several countries, particularly with inter-company transactions.

TRANSFER PRICING VS CUSTOMS VALUE

Companies that are part of the same group might want to transfer inventory between their foreign divisions. In fact, 60 per cent of global trade is made of inter-company shipments. For instance, a corporation might want to establish a distribution centre that will hold inventory for several plants located across several countries. When needed, goods will be transferred from the distribution centre to the various plants across the region. In this case of inter-company transfers, the firm will be selling inventory to itself. There is no transaction price. The value is the transfer price. The transfer price is therefore the value at which goods and services are transferred between two related entities. For the trader the risk comes from the fact that valuation methods for Customs and transfer pricing are not only different, they are conflicting.

Transfer prices can be used to move profit from high to low tax jurisdictions therefore attracting Customs attention. The global fragmentation of production allows companies to consolidate functions generating the most profit, usually intellectual property (IP), in low tax countries. A group could migrate the ownership of IP rights (trademarks, patents, formulas...) to a low tax jurisdiction, for instance Switzerland, from where it charges royalties to the rest of the group for using its IP. This increases the buying price (and import value) in all high tax countries. The selling price remaining the same, this reduces the profit, the taxable base and therefore the tax due.

The profit from IP is reported in Switzerland and taxed at the local rate. At the group level, the profit allocation results in substantial savings. For governments this represents a loss of revenue. In response they introduced complex transfer pricing regulations supported by very high penalties.

In reality, a global supply chain might genuinely cross some low tax locations and the business might be in a position to maximize its tax position. Many multinational companies use transfer pricing regulations to structure their global operations with the objective to build an efficient global tax supply chain. A company sourcing across Asia might want to centralize procurement in Hong Kong and transfer to this central purchasing a whole range of responsibilities: sourcing across the region, selling and delivering the inventory to the rest of the group, managing after sales services, owning the risk of obsolescence and maybe IP rights.

The procurement centre will buy goods across the region and then re-sell them to its worldwide divisions at the transfer price. The transfer price will include the value of the goods purchased across the region plus an additional charge to reflect all the services it provides and the risks it takes.

When transfer pricing applies, Customs risk comes from the difference in valuation methods. The finance department might have designed and implemented a compliant and transparent transfer pricing policy to transfer the inventory between the Hong Kong procurement centre and the rest of the group. The transfer price is likely to be high to reflect all the services and responsibilities handled by the procurement centre. However, at the same time, in the US and in the EU, import departments using Customs valuation method are unbundling the costs to separate the dutiable costs from the non-dutiable to reduce the taxable base. Of course, behind this simple description hides an ocean of complexity and uncertainty. This discrepancy between the two values declared will be spotted during a Customs audit, an internal revenue audit or as it is increasingly happening a combined audit. Penalties are usually very punitive.

In most businesses, international flow of goods usually relies on a physical supply chain designed to benefit from logistics efficiencies and an international transport infrastructure. However, in a company where business restructuring has taken place the physical supply chain could follow corridors and processes to support the tax supply chain.

Transfer pricing, a by-product of globalization, is a relatively new, constantly evolving and extremely complex area of tax with a great impact on Customs valuation. However, authorities have recognized the difficulty that these two sets of valuations creates and the WCO and OECD are jointly working on the convergence of transfer pricing and Customs valuation.

VALUATION AS A SOURCE OF OPPORTUNITY

Customs authorities often offer valuation advice as well as valuation binding rulings. Like for classifications a Customs ruling will add predictability to the clearance process by defining the valuation of the goods that can be used at any Customs office across the Customs territory.

Beside the 'first sale' rule when available, the main opportunity presented by Customs valuation is the reduction of the taxable base under the transaction value method. The process of unbundling will result in removing some costs that might be included in the price but are not subject to duty.

The Customs Valuation Agreement lists costs that when identified separately from the price actually paid or payable can be excluded from the transaction value:

- Buying commissions.

- Charges for the construction, erection, assembly, maintenance or technical assistance undertaken after importation.

- Cost of transport after importation.

It is therefore important for procurement and sales to consider, if possible, valuation when they prepare their costing, quotations and purchase orders. The objective is to ensure visibility of these costs elements to be able to remove them during the valuation process.

QUICK CHECK

Does the business know the 'price actually paid or payable' for its goods?

Has the business obtained a valuation ruling for the Customs authorities?

Does the business purchase or sell goods from or to a related party?

Preferential Rules of Origin and Trade Agreements

A trade agreement signed between countries will deliver substantial advantages to traders in both countries in the form of reduced or nil Customs duties. These preferential rates of duty are not available to other trading nations; they are the privileged of the two countries signatory of the trade agreement.

For instance, as part of the new Japan–Switzerland trade agreement implemented in 2009, countries have granted each other reduced rates of duty. A Swiss manufacturer of umbrellas can now export its products to Japan duty free. However, across the Swiss border, EU manufacturers of umbrellas selling to Japan are subject to the full import duty rate of 4.3 per cent as the EU doesn't have such an agreement with Japan. It would be tempting for all EU manufacturers of umbrellas to truck their product to Switzerland and ship them from there to benefit from the zero percent duty at import in Japan. This is where the preferential rules of origin come into play. They are designed to prevent this kind of trans-shipments and trade diversion.

The objective of preferential rules of origin is to ensure that the product exported and benefiting from a reduced or nil rate of duty is actually produced or manufactured in the country from where it is exported. It is quite easy in the case of vegetables or products that are mined or harvested, for instance. They qualified as 'wholly produced' in a country. It is more difficult for goods manufactured or produced in the country. The wording is vague. It could allow, for instance, some EU umbrellas manufacturers to truck their products in kit or in parts across the border into Switzerland for a simple assembly. Would that be considered as processing? The rules of origin are addressing this issue by defining in great detail what is conferring origin and what isn't. The concept of origin is the cornerstone of all trade agreements. Preferential rules of origin are therefore a set of rules used to determine the nationality of a product. In all trade agreements rules of origin have two parts. The first part covers general provisions applying to all products containing, for instance, the description of rules of origin, certification and direct shipment requirements. The second part contains specific rules applicable to certain HS codes. When goods match the rules of origin they are 'originating goods' and when they don't they are 'non-originating'. Originating goods qualify for preferential treatment that is often a reduced or nil rate of duty. There are three main methods to determine the origin of a product.

CHANGE IN TARIFF CLASSIFICATION

Also called the tariff shift method, this method requires that the imported products or components used in production have a different HS code than the finished products to be exported. This indicates that the imported materials have been sufficiently transformed in the country to obtain origin. Depending on the trade agreement and the intention of the negotiators, the requested change in classification can be based on several levels of the HS: chapter (two digits); heading (four digits); subheading (six digits).

For instance, the North American Free Trade Agreement (NAFTA) specific rules of origin for:

> 9201 Pianos, including automatic pianos; harpsichords and other keyboard stringed.

require that:

> 'Non-originating part should be subject to a change to heading from any other chapter.'

When the change in classification is set at the subheading level, the rules of origin will be easier for a manufacturer than if the tariff shift is at heading or chapter level. The higher the level of change, the more difficult and probably expensive it will be for a manufacturer to comply. Therefore the level of change will indicate the degree of restrictiveness of the agreement. The change in classification can be positive when it describes the change required to confer origin or it can be negative when it covers changes that will not.

This method has the benefit of being very simple for manufacturers to implement. The record keeping does not put any heavy requirement on the business, as most of the information will already be collected for Customs compliance.

SPECIFIC MANUFACTURING PROCESS

The change of classification is not suitable to all products. Some goods might be changing classification without substantial transformation while others undergoing substantial changes might remain in the same heading. The specific manufacturing process corrects this weakness by specifying exactly which type of manufacturing or processing will confer origin.

For instance the US–Morocco trade agreement contains this very demanding requirement for ignition wiring sets and other wiring sets of a kind used in vehicles, aircraft or ships:

8544 30 A change to an ignition wiring set or other wiring set of 8544.30, of a kind used in vehicles, from any other subheading, or from a good within that subheading, provided that assembly of the wiring set involves at least each of the following operations:

a) assembly of at least 10 separate parts;

b) cutting of wire into different lengths to create wire sub-assemblies;

c) stripping of the sheathing of wire;

d) inserting connectors to the ends of wire sub-assemblies;

e) attaching wire sub-assemblies to cable; and

f) 100 per cent testing of wiring sets and other quality control operations and packaging and labelling of finished product.

This method can also be positive by describing processes that will confer origin or negative covering processes that won't.

Under this method manufacturers know exactly how to comply with the terms of the agreement. However, difficulties might arise when introducing changes in the manufacturing process such as new machinery or new processes. At a country level, this method is likely to attract or retain manufacturers wishing to trade under the preferential terms of the agreement.

VALUE ADDED CONTENT

The change in classification and the specific manufacturing process are concerned with the treatment of the goods to determine origin. The value added content rule demands the identification of both the value of the imported materials and the value produced in the country. It is quite common for manufacturers to use in their production some material or components sourced from foreign suppliers. For instance, a piano might be manufactured in Switzerland but some parts might be coming from China. The added-value rules of origin will address the balance between local content (originating) coming from Switzerland and foreign input (non-originating) imported from China. The value added rule will limit the value of non-originating materials used in the exported product.

For instance in the EU–Switzerland rules of origin for a piano:

Chapter 92 – Musical instruments.

Manufacture in which the value of all the non-originating materials used does not exceed 40 per cent of the ex-works price of the product.

Should the Swiss piano manufacturer wishes to sell its piano to the EU under the EU–Swiss trade agreement providing a zero per cent duty rate, than the Ex-work Switzerland price can't have more than 40 per cent of the non-originating materials, in this example, parts coming from China.

The added-value content is the most difficult method to implement because of the many elements that enter into the calculation of origin. This rule has several basis for calculation such as: ex-works price, transaction value, Fob export, factory cost (Estevadeordal and Suominen 2004). For the Swiss piano manufacturer planning to sell to the EU, the ExWork price refers to the transaction value that is the price paid or payable for the goods.

This method needs precise costing information from a cost-based accounting system to identify cost separately. Therefore procurement sourcing abroad under the terms of a trade agreement will have to be confident that their supplier has the capabilities to provide such costing if required. In the same way, the sales team, before selling under the terms of a trade agreement, will have to ensure that internally, the finance department can provide this cost accounting. In addition, costing information must be reviewed regularly as an originating product can, under a change of circumstance, become non-originating.

This method can also be very difficult to manage because the calculation relies in a large part on variable costs. Changes in costs can change the origin status of the goods. For instance, an increase in price of raw material, such as oil or iron ore, can confer origin to some products that previously would not be originating. In the same way, a decrease in exchange rate can decrease the value of some parts and result in the product losing its originating status.

This method is of particular importance for procurement because it affects sourcing and outsourcing decisions. Cost structure will be different between countries and the same product can be originating in one country and not in another. This sometimes can be corrected by postponement techniques where part of the manufacturing process is finished in high wage country, close to the consumer market, to ensure goods will be originating. The value added method can be more or less restrictive. By limiting the amount of foreign content it can, for instance, favour local manufacturers. Under this method, any restructuring of the supply chain or change in sourcing strategy can tilt the delicate balance of origin.

Trade agreements use any of these three methods to determine origin or a combination of them. Furthermore, common to all trade agreements are provisions that negotiators can choose to include:

CUMULATION

Trading partners can use for production any product originating in any of the country signatory of the agreement and retain origin of the exported product.

For instance, a Swiss watchmaker could use parts from a Japanese manufacturer and the Swiss watch shipped to Japan would still be of Swiss origin. Almost all preferential trade agreements include cumulation.

DIAGONAL CUMULATION

Similar to cumulation, it applies to countries part of a group that uses common rules of origin such as the EU Pan-Euro-Med Agreement. Manufacturers can use any product originating from any country in the group and still retain the originating status of the goods.

FULL CUMULATION

An extension of diagonal cumulation where the processing done in any country of the group is carried forward and is counted as if it had been carried in the last country of production. Full cumulation offers a great sourcing advantage to businesses.

TOLERANCE OR DE MINIMIS

This is present in most rules of origin and allows a small amount of non-originating materials to be used without affecting the origin status. Tolerance does not apply to the value content.

DUTY DRAWBACK

Duty drawback allows the manufacturer to claim back, at the time of export, the duty paid on imported goods used in the production process. In many trade agreements duty drawback is not allowed.

OTHER MATERIALS

Packing, accessories, spares parts, sets, tools also have specific conditions to determine their origin.

EXCLUSIONS

Most trade agreements contain a list of non-qualifying operations that can't confer origin such as:

- Changes of packing and breaking-up and assembly of packages.

- Simple painting and polishing operations.

- Simple placing in bottles, cans, flasks, bags, cases or boxes, simple fixing on cards or boards and all affixing or printing marks, labels, logos and other like distinguishing signs on products or their packaging.

- Simple assembly of parts of articles to constitute a complete article or disassembly of products into parts.

RULES OF ORIGIN AS A SOURCE OF RISK

RISK FOR CUSTOMS AUTHORITIES

The risk for Customs is the loss of revenue due to product entering the country under the terms of a trade agreement without being entitled to benefit from that agreement. Monitoring trade agreements presents a challenge for Customs authorities. The multiplication of trade agreements resulted, for the same product, in a multitude of rules of origin as well as different certification requirements. This can also be the source of different interpretations. At export, Customs have to verify the origin of the goods to issue the origin certificate while ensuring that the shipment is not delayed unnecessarily. This might be difficult in the case of complex rules of origin where plural criteria are used demanding detailed costs accounting.

FOR THE IMPORTER

To prove that the products comply with the rules of origin and obtain preferential duty rates, the importer must present a certificate of origin. Unfortunately, this document does not remove Customs risk, at least not for the importer. The exporter must apply for a certificate of origin issued by Customs in the country of export. In practice, many trade agreements allow self-certification for approved exporters. Manufacturers who are approved exporters will therefore prepare a certificate of origin to accompany the goods. The certificate can also take the form of an origin declaration which is a standard sentence printed on the commercial invoice. It is therefore critical that the buyer be completely confident that the supplier can satisfy the rules of origin of a trade agreement. Customs in the country of import will, on presentation of the certificate of origin, apply the preferential duty rate.

However, in case of doubt, discrepancy or as a result of a risk profile they will verify the origin. They will ask Customs authorities of the exporting country to conduct a verification of the manufacturer's records. Should the manufacturer fail to provide all supporting evidence as required by the agreement, for instance detailed costing, then Customs in the country of import will raise an assessment on the importer to collect the duty unpaid. Customs will assess the duties and taxes on all previous shipments for which the manufacturer cannot produce evidence of origin. Although it is the exporter's responsibility to ensure products comply with the rules of origin, it is the importer who carries the risk. Some businesses include in their procurement contract or purchase order a clause to be able to recover the duty charged by Customs as a result of an origin audit. However, the non-compliance will remain against the importer track record.

The logistics of the goods might have to be adapted to satisfy the rules of origin. In many trade agreements there is a requirement for direct shipment of the goods. In such a case the goods must travel directly between the two countries to benefit from the terms of the agreement. The importer must therefore ensure that the supplier and the carrier are aware of the requirement. The trade agreement might also specify that if the business uses identical products, some being originating and other not, they might need to be physically separated in the warehouse. Should this not be possible, the accounting system must be able to separate these two inventories.

FOR THE MANUFACTURER

Each trade agreement has its own rules of origin. A business trading globally will have to comply with several sets of rules. A Swiss chocolate manufacturer selling to the EU and to Japan will have to comply with two sets of rules of origin for the Swiss–EU and Swiss–Japan trade agreements:

Rules of origin for Chapter 18 – Cocoa and Cocoa preparations

Swiss–EU

Manufacture in which all the materials used are classified within a heading other than that of the product; and the value of all the materials of Chapter 17: sugars and sugar confectionery used does not exceed 30 per cent of the ExWorks price of the product.

Swiss–Japan

Change of tariff heading and the maximum value of the non-originating materials classified under Chapter 4: Dairy produce; birds' eggs; natural honey; edible products of animal origin, not elsewhere specified or included and Chapter 17: sugars and sugar confectionery used in the production is 45 per cent of the ExWorks price of the product.

When a business has to comply with several rules of origin, Customs risk affects several departments:

- *Sourcing*: procurement might need to develop different strategies to satisfy both sets of rules of origin. It could, for instance have to source some materials locally instead of buying from its main foreign supplier to ensure the finished goods will satisfy the origin criteria. This could increase the cost of the good sold.

- *Manufacturing*: one of the consequences of rules of origin is the increase of the production cost. This can be the result of imposing certain processes or because economies of scale might not be possible if a production run is required for the US and another for the EU, for instance. Under certain circumstances companies might choose to relocate a process or a plant to comply with the rules of origin. Rules of origin have therefore an impact on foreign direct investment.

- *Finance*: the finance department must have the tools, skills and time to manage costs separately for two or several trade agreements.

- *Sales*: the rules of origin can act as a hidden protection for certain industry and can therefore exclude certain products from a market. The protection might be to support a national policy toward a certain industry or the result of a successful lobbying from national companies. Consequently, the presence of a trade agreement does not necessary mean improved trade terms, although it often does. The degree of Customs risk will be proportional to the restrictiveness of the rules of origin. Whether a business should trade under the terms of a trade agreement is a decision that will affect the risk management.

In some cases, it might not be possible to satisfy both sets of rules at the same time.

The determination of whether a product is originating or not will depend on how the rules of origin are built so the trade is usually very active in lobbying policy makers. Industries have always sought to influence the rules at the negotiation stage. Lobbying has in the past produced very effective rules of origin designed to protect domestic markets from foreign products. However, with the effect of globalization, the trade started manufacturing abroad these goods that now must enter these domestic markets that have been protected by the very restrictive rules of origin that the trade has originally help designed. The trend is changing and the trade is increasingly drawing attention to the complexity and risk in applying rules of origin.

Rules of origin can be quite complicated to implement and monitor. This can discourage some traders from using a trade agreement. Available evidence suggests that traders sometimes prefer to use other Customs procedures or simply pay the duties. Furthermore, the cost of complying might be high. However, in some industries, such as clothing or automotive, that are usually subject to high duty rates, trading under the terms of a trade agreements is a necessity so Customs risk has to be mitigated by sound processes and controls.

RULES OF ORIGIN AS A SOURCE OF OPPORTUNITY

Some Customs authorities provide origin rulings assuring the business with a degree of predictability. However, the main opportunity is the savings generated by the low or nil duty rates. Despite the compliance cost, especially if the rules of origin are not restrictive, using a trade agreement will generate savings. This is particularly true if the product is subject to high duty rate and even more if it is high value.

A trade agreement can also provide a good competitive advantage. For instance, in the competition between Swiss and Belgium chocolate on the Japanese market, the Swiss chocolate has a competitive advantage as a result of the Swiss– Japan trade agreement.

There is a wide choice of trade agreements and often in the same region there might be a competing point of entry of the goods according to the various trade agreements.

In the EU, the rules of origin have been harmonized under The Pan-Euro-Mediterranean Agreement signed between the EU and its trading partners. In the US, the North America Free Trade Agreement (NAFTA) is the blueprint for most other US, Canadian and Mexican trade agreements. In Asia, there is a mixture of rules as the region has been under several influences. The NAFTA rules of origin are used for trade agreements with the US and the Pan-Euro-Med rules for agreement, signed with the EU. At the same time, Asian nations have been very active in signing bilateral agreements with each other using various rules of origin. This could create a very confusing trading environment. However, there are some indications that countries in the region are conscious of this risk and are addressing the issue.

GENERAL SYSTEMS OF PREFERENCE (GSP)

Developed countries, such as the EU, Japan or the US provide these preferences unilaterally to developing countries. Under the GSP scheme, traders in developing country can export their products to a developed country at a reduced or nil rate of duty. However, various GSP schemes apply different rules of origin.

In addition, developed countries have a series of trade preference programs. The US, for instance, has:

- The African Growth and Opportunity Act (AGOA).

- The Andean Trade Preference Act (ATPA).

- The Caribbean Basin Economic Recovery Act (CBERA).

QUICK CHECK

Does the business have a procedure to produce, collect, verify and maintain accurate and complete documentation to substantiate its origin claim?

Does the business have a procedure to check origin compliance of suppliers?

Has the business obtained an origin ruling for the Customs authorities?

⑥ Customs Procedures

Customs procedures are the various methods available to traders to clear goods through Customs. The procedure is selected according to the trader's intended use of the goods. The various Customs procedures present different levels of risk. However, they are also a tool for strategic planning as some procedures can generate cash flow efficiencies and substantial savings.

CUSTOMS PROCEDURES AS A SOURCE OF RISK

From Customs perspective, Customs procedures present various levels of risk that can affect compliance, revenue and security. For the trade, the risk is non-compliance, paying too much duty and missing saving opportunities and efficiencies.

When goods are presented at Customs the trader will, as part of the Customs declaration, select a Customs procedure. The procedure will inform the Customs authorities of the trader's preferred treatment of the goods. For instance, the trader might want to temporary import or export a product for an exhibition.

The importer or exporter is likely to be the declarant (importer/ exporter of records). The declarant is responsible for providing accurate information and paying the required duties and taxes. This is a common source of risk and non-compliance when a business fails to understand that the broker or the agent is acting on behalf of the importer. The agent or broker is only responsible if it clears goods in their own name.

Most imported goods are cleared under 'Home Use', the standard Customs procedure. It applies to goods that are imported to stay within the Customs territory. These goods are therefore subject to duties and taxes. Until the duties and taxes are collected the goods are under Customs control. Once the duties and taxes have been paid, the goods are in 'free circulation' and the traders can dispose of them as they wish. The WCO defines free circulation as 'goods which may be disposed of without Customs restriction'.

At export, most goods are exported under the 'Outright Exportation' procedure also known as definitive export. This procedure is defined in the RKC as 'the Customs procedure applicable to goods which, being in free circulation, leave the Customs territory and are intended to remain permanently outside it'.

The clearance process is a source of risk as it can simply stop the supply chain. Goods have to be declared during opening hours. This seems obvious but there is a risk that an urgent shipment could be sitting on a dock waiting for Customs to open after a public holiday. Opening days and hours will vary between countries and even between cities, for instance, in Hong Kong Customs are opened 24 hours for clearance. A small Customs office is likely to be opened only during office hours. This can affect the speed at which the goods are released, especially if they need to be inspected. Some Customs offices have an out of hours facility usually available at a charge. But most modern Customs authorities accept import declarations before the arrival of the goods. Using risk management, Customs can clear the goods before they have actually been unloaded reducing the risk of delay. If an urgent shipment is going for inspection, the importer or the agent should inform Customs of the urgent nature of the goods. Customs inspect goods in order of urgency starting with live animals and perishables such as food and flowers. So a box containing a resistor will not be at the top of the list. If the resistor is expected to restart a whole production line, then it is likely to be inspected quicker.

Authorizations are an important source of risk. Customs procedures that provide financial benefits to the trade will be subject to authorization because usually what is a financial benefit for the trader is a risk for Customs. These authorizations are very likely to be specific in their description of the processes and activities authorized. It is very easy to lose sight of the content of the authorization. As the market changes and new products are introduced it is not uncommon to use the authorization for a non-authorized usage. For instance, a Customs warehouse authorization will specify exactly which HS codes can be stored. As the business activity evolves, staff change, traders might use the Customs warehouse for non-authorized goods. In addition, many Customs authorizations, declarations and certifications require a signatory. The person might have left the company and still be recorded as the official signatory. A regular review of authorizations to ensure they reflect the current level and nature of business is necessary to mitigate this risk.

CUSTOMS DUTIES

Paying too much or not enough duty is a source of risk although for different reasons. Monitoring the amount of duty paid can help identify areas where duty is unnecessary paid and could be reduced or removed by an appropriate Customs procedure. Paying not enough duty is obviously a non-compliance and an indication of an error in the information declared.

Duties are measured and collected using two types of tariff. Each country has a set of 'bound tariff' and 'applied tariff'. The bound tariff is fixed and is the maximum duty rate that a country can apply to its WTO trading partners. That is to say most of the world trading nations except a few countries and Russia. Members of the WTO must treat all trading partners equally, except in the case of a trade agreement. Under the principle of the Most-Favoured-Nation (MFN), if they grant a low duty rate to one country they must grant it to all countries. The MFN principle is the first article of the General Agreement on Tariffs and Trade (GATT), the set of rules of international trade. Bound tariffs are the result of multilateral negotiations such as the current Doha Round or are agreed when a country joins the WTO such as China in 2001. Bound tariffs are fixed.

The applied tariff is the actual duty rate charged at import. The applied tariff can be the same as the bound tariff but in practice, it is often lower and can vary. When Customs and the trade refer to a duty rate, they always refer to the applied tariff. All WTO members have the obligation to publish their Duty rates which can usually be consulted on the national Customs website. However, it is important for traders to be aware of both tariffs for their products. Simply because a trade dispute or a wave of protectionism can push the applied tariff to the level of the bound tariff. If the difference is small the effect on the business will be insignificant. If the gap between both tariffs is substantial and the industry affected is sensitive or protected, or can be the subject of dispute such as agriculture, then a sudden increase in applied tariff can affect the business objectives.

At the conclusion of the Doha round, a wide range of products is likely to see their bound and applied tariffs decrease, some to zero per cent. Therefore the conclusion of the Doha Round of negotiations, will be a time of intense activities for companies trading globally to check the impact of the agreement on their tariff position. If the tariff of a product that is traded under a trade agreement is reduced to zero per cent then the business might not need to continue with the current arrangement. The business will be able to source from a different location and more generally reorganize its global supply chain.

Duty are expressed in two ways. Ad valorem duties are a percentage of the import value. Specific duties are a fixed amount applied to quantities.

Additional duties are used as part of countries trade defence mechanisms. Anti-dumping duties, countervailing duties and import quotas are usually very specific and temporary. However, they can be implemented rather quickly and the importer might not have time to find an alternative sourcing location. Certain countries and industries are particularly subject to these trade remedies, however they can affect every sector and can therefore pose a risk.

If the imported goods are purchased in a foreign currency the amount of duty paid will be fluctuating according to exchange rates.

While duties are the result of multilateral trade negotiations, taxes are the result of independent domestic fiscal policy. Customs are simply collecting taxes on behalf of other agencies.

CUSTOMS PROCEDURES AS A SOURCE OF OPPORTUNITY

Customs procedures are covered by the Revised Kyoto Convention (RKC) ensuring a minimum of common practices worldwide. However, Customs procedures are part of the RKC Specific Annexes and are therefore not mandatory. This explains why some procedures are available in some countries and not in others. But because in the RKC a country that has accepted a specific annex or chapter is bound by its standards, Customs procedures are, principle at least, harmonized. The names of the procedures covered hereafter are based on the RKC and therefore will be recognised by Customs authorities worldwide. However, in some countries the terminology will be different for historic reason. In the same way, if the spirit and principles of these procedures are common worldwide, there will be differences in their scope and method of implementation between countries. The understanding of their purpose and characteristics will have to be completed with the local requirements.

SIMPLIFIED PROCEDURES

Many Customs authorities have simplified procedures allowing the clearance of the goods against the provision of just a few data for the initial Customs declaration. The trader provides supplementary information necessary to finalize the declaration at a later stage. Certain Customs authorities allow the trader to report all transactions in a single monthly reporting, and even assess their own duties and taxes. Simplified procedures are not available to all traders and are subject to authorization and audit.

Customs duties provide revenue to government and protection to certain industries in the domestic market. As a consequence, they affect the bottom line. They are collected whether the business sells the goods it imports or not and whether the business makes a profit or not. However, there are many instances where imported goods do not remain in the domestic market. If duties are collected on goods that will be subsequently exported, they will increase the cost of the goods sold and will damage the business position on export markets. Several Customs procedures are available to correct these effects.

CUSTOMS WAREHOUSING

The RKC defines Customs warehousing as a 'procedure under which imported goods are stored under Customs control in a designated place (a Customs warehouse) without payment of import duties and taxes'.

Goods entered into this Customs procedure have not yet been imported. They are on the Customs territory but duties and taxes have not been paid so they are under Customs control.

Consequently, traders can't use the goods as they wish. The procedure, also known as bonded warehouse, will result in the goods entering a warehouse at a specific location that can be, for instance, at the carrier or the trader premises. The Customs warehouse can, in some countries, be a part of the trader general warehouse.

Approval has to be obtained from Customs and there might be a time limit for the goods to stay in the warehouse. Customs will require at a minimum a guarantee, a safe location with security equipments, such as an alarm, and sound inventory control and accounting processes and systems.

The Customs warehousing procedure will be closed when goods are removed from the warehouse and declared into another Customs procedure such as Home Use.

A Customs warehouse can be an added-value service for many different business functions.

Under this procedure traders can't process the goods, however, they can carry out a range of tasks such as operations necessary to protect the good or to keep them in good condition. Products might be sorted and repacked, for instance, to combine two different products in the same packaging to satisfy a promotional offer organized by the sales department. In many countries labelling can be carried out under this procedure. This allow a business to consolidate the inventory of unlabelled products and delay the labelling with the language of the country of destination until customer requirements are known. Furthermore, goods can be exported to another country or returned to the factory without having paid duties and taxes. In some countries, kitting and even light manufacturing is authorized allowing traders to make slight adjustments to the goods close to the consumer market.

This procedure can also be used by procurement in a strategic buy ahead initiative when they buy goods in higher quantities than necessary to benefit from favourable exchange rates. Sales can be interested in the procedure when they need to leave some inventory of material or spare parts close to their customer's site such as a Vendor Managed Inventory.

Financially, this procedure is beneficial for the cash flow as it can delay the tax point and the payment of duty and taxes. In case of fluctuation of the exchange rate, the choice of date of removing goods can generate exchange rate efficiencies. In certain countries goods can be revalued under this procedure. This is very important for seasonal products and perishable or fashion items where the price of the goods decreases as the season progresses.

When used in conjunction with other procedures, Customs warehouse can provide additional benefits.

Under the drawback procedure traders can obtain a refund of import duties and taxes when goods are exported. Using the Customs warehousing procedure will allow the trader to receive a refund as soon as goods enter the Customs warehouse. This gives the trader the possibility to consolidate export orders to benefit from better transport rates while getting refunds of duties and taxes quicker.

In the EU the type 'E' Customs warehouse is a virtual warehouse where the business inventory control systems track the movement and usage of goods that are stored in various physical warehouses across several countries in the EU.

However, if the Customs warehousing procedure is not considered in relation to the global supply chain, it might deliver unwanted results. Introducing a Customs warehouse to serve several countries and centralize regional distribution can be an attractive option. From a logistics point of view, the distribution centre will generate economies of scale. However, it might also affect the fragile balance of origin. Products purchased or sold under the terms of a trade agreement are subject to the rules of direct shipment. Products routed via the regional distribution centre will loose their originating status. As a result they will not be entitled to enter the final consumers market at a reduced or nil rates of duty. For products subject to high duty rates, particularly if high value, introducing a regional customs warehouse could have a negative effect.

DRAWBACK

Drawback is the Customs procedure that allows the refund of duties collected at import on a product that is subsequently exported or destroyed. According to the RKC drawback is a procedure which: 'when goods are exported, provides for a repayment (total or partial) to be made in respect of the import duties and taxes charged on the goods, or on materials contained in them or consumed in their production'.

Drawback is a very common procedure available in most countries. It is subject to authorization and the record keeping must show a full audit trail following the product from import to export. If the goods are destroyed Customs will specify whether a certificate is required. Under certain authorizations the same product must be returned, others accept the exchange of similar products.

Drawback is the procedure that perhaps has the most different interpretations worldwide while, at the same time, keeping in line with the RKC. The RKC states that 'National legislation shall enumerate the cases in which drawback may be claimed'. As the consequence drawback is used in many different cases. In the US, there are different types of drawback covering a wide range of activities such as unused-merchandise drawback, or rejected-merchandise drawback.

The inconvenience of drawback is that the trader has to finance the duties and taxes while the product is on the Customs territory affecting the cash flow and working capital. The impact on the business will depend on the value, duty rate and volume of goods imported and the length of the manufacturing process. The longer the process the more expensive it might be to finance the duty and taxes. Other economic factors that will impact on drawback are high interest rates and inflation. Furthermore, drawback is specifically forbidden in most trade agreements.

The procedure is closed with the export of the finished products, the transfer to a Customs warehousing procedure or a free trade zone. Entering the goods into the Customs warehouse procedure or into a free trade zone will trigger the refund of duties and taxes.

INWARD PROCESSING

This procedure is similar to drawback with the added advantage that duties and taxes are not paid upfront but suspended. This procedure is used by traders to suspend import duties on goods that will be processed, manufactured into a finished product then subsequently exported. It can also be used to suspend duties on a product that will be repaired before being re-exported. The RKC defines inward processing as a procedure under which 'certain goods can be brought into a Customs territory conditionally relieved from payment of import duties and taxes, on the basis that such goods are intended for manufacturing, processing or repair and subsequent exportation'.

In practice, import duties and taxes are suspended at import until the goods are exported therefore no payment is required. In the EU this procedure has two versions: Inward Processing Drawback and Inward Processing Suspension.

The procedure applies to traders intending to export part or all of the goods and it is subject to authorization. There is a time limit for the throughput period. The trader often has the choice of applying for an authorization that will cover just one specific shipment or a blanket authorization for regular transactions. The authorization will detail the terms under which the procedure is applicable. It will cover the goods involved, the processing, the quantity, the rate of yield and the finished products. Record keeping must link the imported and exported products and provide a full audit trail although the level and detail of record keeping requirement will vary by country. Record keeping is likely to be heavier than for goods imported under drawback because duties and taxes have not been paid so the risk for Customs to lose revenue is higher. The trader will have to keep detailed records to track the imported product through the manufacturing process from inventory of raw material, WIP, finished goods to by-products. Customs also often requires regular reporting. The procedure has to be closely managed because the manufacturing activity can change and impact on the authorization, for instance, the introduction of a new process or a change in the bill of material. Goods can enter inward processing directly at import or be transferred from the Customs warehousing or Customs transit procedure. The procedure is closed with the export of the finished products, the transfer to a Customs warehouse or a free trade zone. If some products are not re-exported they will be entered under the Home Use procedure and import duties and taxes will be collected.

This procedure produces savings and cash flow efficiencies, however, it might not be compatible with the terms of trade agreements. It is effective to produce economies of scale by centralizing the manufacturing of products for a whole region. The objective of inward processing is to encourage domestic manufacturing.

Inward processing is a very common procedure used by most multinational organization with multiple manufacturing centres. It is the driver behind the concept of the global factory where goods travel between plants for further processing until they are transferred to a Customs warehouse waiting for customers orders. The fact that, in some countries, the manufacturer does not have to own the goods gives businesses the possibility of outsourcing some or all of the manufacturing while retaining ownership of the inventory.

OUTWARD PROCESSING

This procedure is the opposite of Inward Processing. The RKC defines Outward Processing as a Customs procedure: 'under which goods which are in free circulation in a Customs territory may be temporarily exported for manufacturing, processing or repair abroad and then re-imported with total or partial exemption from import duties and taxes'.

The procedure is subject to authorization. The authorization can cover one shipment, for instance, a tool sent back to the manufacturer to be repaired or several transactions. The exchange of similar products might be allowed. Record keeping is similar to Inward Processing although often less demanding. The audit trail must follow the product from export to import if possible at the serial number level although for some products the part number level might be sufficient. The procedure is closed when the exported product has been imported. If the business is trading under the terms of a trade agreement, the processing done in the foreign country can affect the fragile balance of originating and non-originating costs under the value-added rule of origin.

PROCESSING GOODS FOR HOME USE

This relatively recent Customs procedure allow traders to calculate import duties on material, parts and components used in manufacturing based on the classification and duty rate of the finished product. It is define in the RKC as a procedure 'under which imported goods may be manufactured, processed or worked, before clearance for Home Use and under Customs control, to such an extent that the amount of the import duties and taxes applicable to the products thus obtained is lower than that which would be applicable to the imported goods'.

This procedure, which is not available in every country, has been designed to correct a tariff anomaly resulting from the decrease in duty rates. Following the various multilateral agreements and the general trends of decrease in Customs duties, some products have become free of duty. However, the materials, parts and components necessary to manufacture these products remained subject to duties. For instance, chemicals and components used to manufacture a semiconductor are subject to duty when the semiconductor itself is duty free. This tariff discrepancy discouraged local production so some countries authorize the parts and components imported to manufacture these products to be taxed at the rate of the finished product. This procedure might not be allowed for businesses trading under the terms of a trade agreement.

This quite complex procedure is subject to authorization and applies to product that will remain in the Customs territory. Similar to Inward Processing it requires a cost accounting system capable to tracking the material used though the manufacturing process. The goods can enter the procedure from a Customs warehouse. The procedure is closed with the goods being declared to Home Use.

This procedure will reduce the cost of the goods sold so products manufactured locally can compete with imported products.

END USE

The end use procedure allows, in some countries, full or partial relief of duty on goods that are destined to a specific industry or a particular use. For instance, in the EU, under this procedure, most aircraft spare parts can be imported at zero per cent duty.

TEMPORARY ADMISSION

This procedure allows good to be imported for a fixed period of time and for a specific purpose. Temporary admission is defined in the RKC as a procedure: 'under which certain goods can be brought into a Customs territory conditionally relieved totally or partially from payment of import duties and taxes; such goods must be imported for a specific purpose and must be intended for re-exportation within a specified period and without having undergone any change except normal depreciation due to the use made of them'.

Under this procedure some products are usually free of duty such as exhibition materials, professional tools and equipment, goods imported for educational, scientific or cultural purposes. Each country will have a list of authorized use.

The procedure is subject to authorization. The procedure is closed when the goods are exported. If the goods are sold while under Temporary Admission, a Customs declaration will have to transfer the goods to the Home Use procedure and the appropriate duties and taxes will have to be paid.

Another way to manage temporary admission is with ATA Carnet. ATA is a mix of French and English meaning '*Admission Temporaire-Temporary Admission*'. It is a simplified international Customs declaration that follows the movement of temporary goods providing duty free import. The exporter needs to set up a bank guarantee that will reduce the risk of loss of revenue for Customs but will affect the business credit line. However, the importer does not have to finance the import duty and taxes providing benefits to the cash flow. The simplicity of the procedure is suited to simple transactions and small exporters.

REIMPORTATION IN THE SAME STATE

This procedure allows traders to import goods returning from abroad free of duty and taxes. Under this procedure any processing or repair done abroad to the goods is not allowed.

This is, for instance, applicable when a foreign customer returns a product.

CUSTOMS TRANSIT

Very often goods have to travel across one or several countries to reach their final destination. This is the case, for instance, when goods are shipped to a country that does not have access to the sea. Customs transit is the procedure that will allow the goods to travel across these countries. Goods travelling under the Customs transit procedure are under Customs supervision and are not subject to the payment of duties. The RKC defines Customs transit as the 'Customs procedure under which goods are transported under Customs control from one Customs office to another'.

Goods under transit can travel by road, rail, air, sea and inland waterways. A set of conditions will be in place to ensure that the shipment will not be diverted without the payment of duty and taxes. These will include a financial guarantee, a time limit and a seal that will be affixed to the transport unit.

The Customs transit procedure can also apply nationally. This is the case, for instance, when a shipment is cleared at the importer local Customs office instead of the port.

Transit by road is simplified further with the use TIR (Transport International Routier) carnets. This procedure allows a truck with goods under transit to cross several borders using a carnet to declare the shipment at each border crossing.

OTHER FACILITIES

Free Trade Zone

A Free Trade Zone (FTZ) is a part of the country that for duties and taxes purposes is considered outside the Customs territory. Consequently, many Customs requirements and procedures do not apply. FTZs are governed by sets of rules that vary between countries and between the zones themselves. Therefore the type of goods, the processing and manufacturing allowed in an FTZ will vary greatly worldwide.

Goods entering a FTZ can be foreign goods arriving from abroad and domestic goods entering from the country where the zone is located. Because a FTZ is outside the Customs territory, domestic goods entering the zone are considered as export. Like a Customs warehouse this can provide a cash flow benefit for goods under drawback, as refund will be received when goods are entering the zone. Goods can leave a FTZ to be shipped abroad or to stay in the country. In that case, they will be entering the Customs territory through the import declaration placed under any Customs procedures.

Payment facilities

Each country collects duties and taxes in accordance with its own procedure and will have its own payment methods and payment dates. In some countries Customs authorities have the facility to defer the payment of duties and taxes against a security instrument such as: deposit, bank guarantee or bond. The security can be in place for a single shipment or for all regular transactions. The facility to defer payment will have a positive effect on the cash flow. In addition, some Customs authorities have payment terms of 30 days. With a 30 days deferment account and 30 days payment terms the import duties will only be due in 60 days. This facility can be very useful for importers of large value items that can import goods at the beginning of the period.

It is likely that the financial guarantee required will be proportionate to the volume of business imported and the amount of duty paid monthly. Therefore the size of the account should be appropriate to the level of import. Should the volume of import decrease, for instance in the case of a change of sourcing, it would be beneficial to review and reduce the level of the account and consequently the guarantee. The guarantee is often part of the business credit line and reducing the guarantee, will reduce the borrowing level and free up some credit available to the business.

SINGLE EUROPEAN AUTHORISATION (SEA)

Businesses trading across several EU countries have to deal with the Customs authority of every country in which they operate. Using a Single European Authorisation (SEA) they can centralise all transactions and payments of duties and taxes in one country. The trader can report all import and export transactions in one country despite several points of entry of the goods across the EU.

The SEA provide several benefits:

- *Strengthen compliance*: all transactions are handled by only one office and Customs reporting is done in one place. It will therefore be easier to implement compliant processes, carry out controls and develop a good relationship with Customs.

- *Generate savings and efficiencies*: the cost of the processing of import and export transactions is centralized in one office instead of being spread across several countries. Furthermore, the local volume of movements in each country might have favoured the use of local agents but the EU wide level of transactions could justify bringing the function internally. This new back office function can, for instance, be part of the remit of a Shared Service Centre.

- *Identify savings opportunities*: as the business gains a detailed vision of all its Customs transactions across the whole EU, some pockets or inefficiencies are likely to appear. It will be easier to fine-tune the supply chain by introducing certain Customs procedures in some part of the territory.

One note of caution, the choice of the country in which to implement the SEA will have an impact on the efficiency of the business. Not all Customs authorities across the EU are equal. Some are more efficient than others.

Many Customs procedures can be a source of competitive advantage, improvement of cash flow and savings. However, 'procedures with economic impact' will demand high level of administration and control. Deciding to use a procedure will be a question of striking the balance between the benefit of the procedure, the cost of implementation and the risk to be managed.

QUICK CHECK

Has the business recently checked that all authorizations are up to date and relevant to the nature and level of business?

Has the business developed processes and controls to ensure compliance with the requirements of specific Customs procedures?

Is the business using Customs planning to maximize efficiencies and savings available from Customs procedures?

(7) Security – The New Challenge

Security has always been part of international trade. Cargo always had to be protected. However, since 9/11 the security focus has changed and while the cargo still needs to be protected, countries think they also need protection from the cargo.

Before 2001, the main focus of most Customs authorities was on revenue collection. The events of 9/11 changed the priorities. Suddenly, the global supply chain could be used to transport weapons as well as being a weapon itself. For instance, to block a critical trade lane or shut down a major port. This sudden focus on security created a series of challenges for Customs administrations. Customs authorities have had to increase their cooperation with other government agencies such as the police, immigration and coast guards. They also had to increase their level of cooperation with their international colleagues. Finally, they had to develop new working relationships with the trade as large parts of the global supply chain belong to or is managed by the private sector. Public–private partnership initiatives have been developed. Some, already existing, have been updated and new one have been created. Under these new conditions, the trade faces two types of Customs risk: security and compliance. Security risk is linked to the trader supply chain being used for illegal activity. With strengthened controls at borders, infiltrating a trader's supply chain can provide a pipeline for all kind of traffic. Compliance risk is the result of an increase in security requirements and regulations.

SECURITY INITIATIVES

Since 2001, a wide number of initiatives have been introduced at national, regional and international level putting new demands on traders. Security initiatives can be mandatory or voluntary. However, those that are voluntary might in practice be mandatory, as businesses increasingly demand from their suppliers a security accreditation.

WCO – SAFE

From a Customs perspective the only international supply chain security standard is the WCO Framework of Standards to Secure and Facilitate Global Trade (SAFE framework) adopted in June 2005. It is a multilateral convention applicable to all operators along the global supply chain as well as Customs authorities and it covers all modes of transports.

SAFE is very much in the spirit of the Revised Kyoto Convention and other WCO instruments as it promotes standardized and harmonized practices. The framework responds to the concern that, after 9/11, each country could be tempted to develop its own trade security initiative; and most countries have. This poses a problem to global traders having to comply with a range of different schemes. It also poses a problem for

Customs authorities as disparate security initiatives complicate collaboration and exchange of information in order to secure the whole of the supply chain. Although the SAFE framework is voluntary, all WCO members have declared their intention to implement SAFE.

The premise for SAFE is that most of international trade is made of legitimate transactions and does not pose a security risk. However, among the volume of trade hides threats from terrorist activities, trafficking, piracy and other illegal activities. The core idea is to use risk management techniques to authorize consignments from compliant traders arriving at the borders and concentrate on the others. This reaches two objectives; facilitating trade for compliant traders and concentrate Customs resources on checking identified risks.

SAFE has four main objectives:

- The harmonization of advance cargo information.

  Checking consignments at import does not protect from an attack designed to close a major trade lane or port facility. Therefore, cargo integrity will increasingly be checked before loading, with the introduction of advance shipping information provided by the trade to Customs. These data will be processed through the risk management system resulting in instruction such as 'load' or 'do not load'. The SAFE framework describes the data to be collected and the process to collect them.

- The use of risk management techniques.

Security measures are based on risk management processes and all Customs authorities should use similar risk targeting method.

- The inspection of outbound cargo upon request of the importing country.

  As a result of the risk management exercise, the importing country can ask the exporting country to inspect the goods. However, under the RKC physical inspections must be done in a way that disrupts the supply chain as least as possible and allow the smooth flow of cargo across borders. Therefore, a wide range of detection equipments has been introduced.

- A partnership with the trade delivering advantages to traders meeting the supply chain security requirements.

To reach these objectives SAFE has 17 detailed standards covering Customs and the trade. These standards are grouped under two pillars: the Customs to Customs pillar covers Customs operations; the Customs to Business pillar manages the relationship between Customs and the trade.

The Customs to Customs pillar contains 11 international standards harmonizing Customs security practices and procedures in terms of:

Standard 1 Integrated Secure Customs Management, securing the whole supply chain.

Standard 2 Cargo inspection authority.

Standard 3 Modern Technology in inspection equipment covers the use of non-invasive equipment.

Standard 4 Risk management systems.

Standard 5 Identification of high-risk cargo or container.

Standard 6 Advance electronics information.

Standard 7 Common and standardized targeting and communication.

Standard 8 Performance measurement.

Standard 9 Security assessment.

Standard 10 Employee integrity.

Standard 11 Outbound security inspection.

The Customs to business pillar organizes the relationship between Customs authorities and the trade. These six international standards include measures to be implemented by the trade to secure the supply chain and cover areas of:

Standard 1 Partnership program.

Standard 2 Security best practices.

Standard 3 Validation and authorization of authorized traders.

Standard 4 Use of technology to maintain cargo security and integrity.

Standard 5 Communication with Customs to promote security.

Standard 6 Facilitation.

The cornerstone of the Customs to Business pillar is the Authorised Economic Operator program (AEO). This accreditation scheme allows companies satisfying a set of security criteria to enter into partnership with Customs. In exchange, businesses have access to faster Customs treatment. SAFE defines the AEO as a:

> *Party involved in the international movement of goods in whatever function that has been approved by or on behalf of a national Customs administration as complying with WCO or equivalent supply chain security standards. Authorised Economic Operator includes inter alias manufacturers, importers, exporters, brokers, carriers, consolidators, intermediates, ports, airports, terminal operators, integrated operators, warehouses, distributors.*

Under SAFE, to become an Authorised Economic Operator a trader must demonstrate:

- Compliance with Customs requirements.

- Satisfactory system for management of commercial records.

- Financial viability.

- Consultation, cooperation and communication.

- Education, training and awareness.

- Information exchange, access and confidentiality.

- Cargo security.

- Conveyance security.

- Premises and personnel security.

- Trading partner security.

- Processes for crisis management and incident recovery.

- Processes for measurement, analysis and improvement.

SAFE is reviewed every three years to evolve in accordance with business practices and world events.

CERTIFICATION PROGRAMS

Certification programs have similarities and differences. Some have been designed and implemented before SAFE so they inherit differences with the standards that should be fading as the programs are aligned. However, there is also a difference in the interpretation of the framework and therefore in its implementation. For instance, in SAFE the AEO accreditation covers importers and exporters while the US Customs and Trade

Partnership Against Terrorism (C-TPAT) covers only importers; C-TPAT focuses mainly on security while in the EU the AEO incorporates trade, fiscal and regulatory requirements. Most countries are now in discussion with their trading partners to recognize each other's accreditation programs and many Customs administrations are signing mutual recognition agreements. This is critical to the trade as a global system is preferable than having to manage several accreditations.

1995 – CANADA PARTNERSHIP IN PROTECTION (PIP)

This Customs-trade program introduced to promote Customs compliance was modified in 2001 to include security issues. The program has seen further transformation to make it compatible with SAFE and C-TPAT in view of mutual recognition. The modernized PIP, was introduced in 2008.

It is voluntary, however, it is compulsory for companies wanting to participate in the Free and Secure Trade Program (FAST). FAST is an agreement between the US, Canada and Mexico to coordinate and harmonize their processes for Customs clearance with dedicated lanes and faster clearance.

1996 – BUSINESS ALLIANCE FOR SECURE COMMERCE (BASC)

This private sector initiative, initially called 'Business Anti-Smuggling Coalition' was designed by the trade to protect shipments from Latin America to the US. In particular from drug smuggling. It is a voluntary program including companies, mainly in Latin America, trading with the US. After 2001, the program has been modified to include security measures.

2001 – USA – CUSTOMS-TRADE PARTNERSHIP AGAINST TERRORISM (C-TPAT)

A voluntary certification program introduced in November 2001 focusing on security. It applies to manufacturers, Customs brokers and carriers but only for imports and for just one mode of transport: sea freight. To be accredited businesses must introduce a series of security measures. They also must conduct a self-assessment of the level of security of the whole global supply chain including trading partners.

There are three levels of certification:

- Tier 1 Certified companies have successfully submitted to Customs a preliminary written assessment of their supply chain security.

- Tier 2 Companies have passed on-site inspections and obtained C-TPAT validation.

- Tier 3 Companies are certified and validated and implement some or all of the best practices suggested by Customs.

C-TPAT although voluntary is mandatory for a company that wants to be certified with the FAST program.

2005 – ISO 28000

Developed by the International Organization for Standardization this voluntary standard helps businesses develop processes for supply chain security. ISO 28000 covers many areas of the business from packing to production but also finance.

2008 – EU – AUTHORISED ECONOMIC OPERATOR

The EU certification program entered into force on 1 January 2008. The EU program covers security as well as Customs and Trade compliance and is recognized in all 27 EU countries. There are three levels of AEO:

AEO Custom's Simplification

This level focuses on compliance. To obtain this accreditation the company, its owner and main shareholders must have been, among other things, compliant with Customs and fiscal regulations for the previous 3 years. An assessment must demonstrate the business financial solvency.

AEO Certificate Security and Safety

This level focuses on security and is in the same spirit of the US C-TPAT but covers exporters and importers.

AEO Certificate Customs Simplification/Security and Safety

This is the combination of two previous levels with the requirements and benefits of both types of AEO.

2008 – CHINA – AUTHORISED ECONOMIC OPERATOR

China's program includes security as well as Customs and Trade compliance requirements. Five levels of classification: AA, A, B, C, D apply to traders and agents and cover import and export. Categories A and AA benefit from trade facilitation measures.

Class A

To be in the Class A category, businesses must have been, among other things, a Class B for 12 months without any non-compliance with Customs and other government agencies. The trader must also have less than 3 per cent errors in Customs declarations. Imports and exports for the previous year must exceed 500,000 USD and the business must have a sound accounting system.

Class AA

Traders must have been a Class A for 12 months. A Customs audit must show compliance in terms of security practices, trade compliance processes and internal control. Businesses will also need to provide regular business and financial reporting as well as information on internal controls. Imports and exports for the previous year must exceed 30 million USD.

ADVANCE CARGO INFORMATION

Advance cargo information is part of SAFE Customs to Customs pillar and allows Customs authorities to received information in advance of the shipment to run risk management checks. This new requirement was introduced in the US in January 2009 with a one-year introductory period during which US Customs have helped the trade adjust to this new demand. In the EU, advance cargo information came into force in July 2009. The advance notification covers import and export. The data elements required varies between means of transport, Customs procedures, and between traders depending on whether they are an authorized operator or not. During the transitional period, imports for which an advance notification has not been received in advance of arrival will be subject to risk assessment after their arrival. The transitional period will end in December 2010. Traders are concerned that the various data and formats required between countries could complicate the collection, management and transmission of information. Especially when goods manufactured at the same factory are shipped to several countries having different data set requirements. Despite the WCO Data Model the are some divergences in data requirements.

US IMPORTER SECURITY FILING AND ADDITIONAL CARRIER REQUIREMENTS (ISF)

Also called the 10+2 rules, the ISF requires that importers or their agent provide eight data elements no later than 24 hours before the cargo is loaded aboard a vessel destined to the United States. Those data elements include:

- Seller.

- Buyer.

- Importer of record number/FTZ applicant identification number.

- Consignee number(s).

- Manufacturer (or supplier).

- Ship to party.

- Country of origin.

- Commodity Harmonized Tariff Schedule of the United States (HTSUS) number.

If possible, these data elements should be collected at the purchase order stage to avoid any delay. A delay can arise from the difficulty to identify the manufacturing plant when, for instance, products are shipped from a centralized warehouse consolidating the production from several plants across a region.

Two additional data elements must be submitted by the shipping line as early as possible, but no later than 24 hours before the ship's arrival at a US port. These data elements are:

- Container stuffing location.

- Consolidator.

QUICK CHECK

Has the business developed a security policy, procedures and controls including security measures based on best practices from national Customs administrations or the SAFE program?

Is the business confident that its supply chain is secure and can't be infiltrated by illegal trade?

Conclusion

The word 'frontier' comes from 'the front', where the army faces the front line. Although this meaning is still applicable to many countries, in most of the world, frontiers have different shapes. The economic frontiers have, for the past 40 years, gone down with the decrease in duty rates. In the meantime, political frontiers have gone up suddenly in 2001. The physical frontier is not the place of all controls anymore. Instead, risk management checks are computerized operations being carried out along the global supply chain in a borderless world.

Customs practices evolve driven by the continuous changes in the level of these frontiers as well as changes in international trade. Fortunately, businesses have the chance to prepare for these changes as new trade agreements and Customs regulations are discussed well in advance of their implementation. Trade publications cover the proposed changes and debates are usually raging across the international trade community. While the business must constantly monitor its trading environment to prepare for the next developments it also needs to keep an eye on internal changes. A new export account, a new foreign supplier, a new product, a change in logistics, an update in transfer pricing can all contribute to Customs risk.

In the meantime, under the auspice of the WCO, Customs authorities are continually harmonizing their working practices and data management, slowly building a globally integrated Customs network that might ultimately oversee a global border.

References

JOURNAL ARTICLES

Appeals, T. and Struye de Swielande, S. 1998. Rolling back the frontiers: the customs clearance revolution. *International Journal of Logistics Management*. Vol 9, No 1, pp. 111–118.

Augier, P., Gasiorek, M. and Lai Tong, C. 2005. The impact of rules of origin on trade flows. *Economic Policy*. Vol 20, No 43, pp. 567–624.

Feichtner, I. 2008. The administration of the vocabulary of international trade: the adaptation of WTO schedules to changes in the Harmonized System. *German Law Journal*. Vol 9, No 11.

Gutiérrez, X., Hintsa, J., Wieser, P. and Hameri, A.P. 2007. Voluntary supply chain security program impact: an empirical study with BASC member companies. *World Customs Journal*. Vol 1, No 2, pp. 31–48.

Haughton, M.A. and Desmeules, R. 2001. Recent reforms in customs administrations. *International Journal of Logistics Management*. Vol 12, No 1, pp. 65–82.

Krishna, K. and Krueger, A.O. 1995. Implementing free trade areas: rules of origin and hidden protection. *National Bureau of Economic Research*. Working Paper No. 4983, Washington.

Ooyevaar, N. and Bennett, A. 2007. Bridging transfer pricing and customs. *International Tax Review*. Vol 18, No 11, p. 26.

Ruessmann, L. and Willems, A. 2009. Revisiting the first sale for export rule: an attempt to remove fairness in the interests of raising revenues, without improving legal certainty. *World Customs Journal*. Vol 3, No 1.

Widdowson, D. 2007. The changing role of Customs: evolution or revolution? *World Customs Journal*. Vol 1, No 1.

WEBSITE/ONLINE MATERIAL

Administration des Douanes et Impôts Indirects Maroc. 2009. Ghrairi. L. *Gestion des règles d'origine par la douane*. Available at: http://www.wcoomd.org.

Asia Pacific Customs News. 2009. *Korea Customs policies in the global economic crisis ISSUE 31*. Available at: http://www. wcoasiapacific.org [accessed: 27 June 2009].

Asia-Pacific Research and Training Network on Trade. 2008. *Trade Facilitation beyond the multilateral trade negotiations: regional practices, Customs valuation and other emerging issues*. Available at: http://www.unescap.org/publications/detail. asp?id=1258 [accessed: 29 July 2009].

CBP. 2004. *An informed compliance publication.* Available at: http://www.cbp.gov.

CBP. 2009. *Trade strategy Fiscal years 2009-2013.* Available at: www.cbp.gov/.../trade/trade.../trade_strategy/...trade_strategy.../cbp_trade_ strategy.pdf [accessed: 2 June 2009].

General Administration of Customs. 2009. Ping, L. *China. preferential rules of origin: what what's new from China?* Available from: http://www.wcoomd.org.

Joann Peterson, J. and Treat, A. 2008. The *Post-9/11 global framework for cargo.* Available at: www.usitc.gov/publications/332/journals/cargo_security.pdf [accessed: 25 May 2009].

Sweden Board of Trade. 2008. *Supply chain security initiatives: a trade facilitation perspective.* Available at: www.kommers.se [accessed: 10 June 2009].

The World Bank. 2005. *Customs modernization handbook.* Available at: siteresources.worldbank.org/.../Customs_Modernization_Handbook.pdf [accessed: 11 April 2009].

UNCTAD. 2008. *Border agency coordination/cooperation.* Available at: http://r0.unctad.org/ttl/technical-notes.htm.

UNCTAD. 2008. *Post-Clearance audit. Technical Note 5.* Available at: http://r0.unctad.org/ttl/technical-notes.htm.

UNCTAD. 2008. *Risk management in Customs procedures. Technical Note 12.* Available at: http://r0.unctad.org/ttl/technical-notes.htm.

UNCTAD. 2008. *Use of customs automation systems. Technical Note 3.* Available at: http://r0.unctad.org/ttl/technical-notes.htm.

TREATIES, CONVENTIONS, AGREEMENTS

Agreement Implementation of Article VII of the General Agreement on Tariffs and Trade. 1994. Geneva: WTO.

Integrate Supply Chain Management Guidelines. 2004. Brussels: WCO.

International Convention on the Harmonized System. 1983. Brussels: WCO.

International Convention on Mutual Administrative Assistance in Customs Matters. 2003. Brussels: WCO.

International Convention on the Simplification and Harmonisation of Customs Procedures (as amended) Revised Kyoto Convention. 1999. Brussels: WCO.

Measures of the General Administration of Customs of the People's Republic of China on Classified Management of Enterprises, January 4, 2008, promulgated by Decree No. 170 of the General Administration of Customs of the People's Republic of China on January 30, 2008, and effective as of April 1, 2008.

Recommended amendments to the Harmonized System Nomenclature to Enter into Force on 1 January 2012 – WCO Council Recommendation of 26 June 2009. Brussels: WCO.

Regulation (EC) No 450/2008 of the European Parliament and of the Council of 23 April 2008 Laying Down the Community Customs Code (Modernised Customs Code). OJ L145/1 4.6.2008.

Regulation (EC) No 450/2008 Laying Down the Community Customs Code [2008] OJ L145/1.

Risk Management Guide. 2003. Brussels: WCO.

WCO SAFE Framework of Standards to Secure and Facilitate Global Trade. 2006. Brussels: WCO.

Text of FTA agreements:

Japan-Switzerland

EU-Japan

US-Morrocco

EU-Switzerland

LAW REPORT

Case C-376/07 *Hoge Raad der Nederlanden (Netherlands) Staatssecretaris van Financiën v Kamino International Logistics BV*. [2009] OJ C90/4.

CONFERENCE PAPERS

Estevadeordal, A. and Suominen, K. 2004. *Rules of Origin: A World Map and Trade Effects*. Paper to The Seventh Annual Conference on Global Economic Analysis: Trade, Poverty and the Environment, The World Bank, Washington, DC, 17–19 June 2004.

Estevadeordal, A., Harris. J. and Suominen, K. 2008. *Multilateralising Preferential Rules of Origin Around the World*. Paper to the WTO/HEI/NCCR Trade/CEPR Conference: Multilateralising Regionalism, Geneva, Switzerland, 10–12 September 2007.

If you have found this book useful you may be interested in other titles from Gower

International Trade and the Successful Intermediary
Davide Giovanni Papa and Lorna Elliott
Hardback: 978-0-566-08934-3
e-book: 978-0-566-09223-7

Just-in-Time Logistics
Kee-hung Lai and T.C.E. Cheng
Hardback: 978-0-566-08900-8
e-book: 978-0-566-09216-9

**The Project Manager's Guide to Purchasing:
Contracting for Goods and Services**
Garth Ward
Hardback: 978-0-566-08692-2
e-book: 978-0-7546-8129-8

**Risk Strategies:
Dialling Up Optimum Firm Risk**
Les Coleman
Hardback: 978-0-566-08938-1
e-book: 978-0-566-08939-8

Visit **www.gowerpublishing.com** and

- search the entire catalogue of Gower books in print
- order titles online at 10% discount
- take advantage of special offers
- sign up for our monthly e-mail update service
- download free sample chapters from all recent titles
- download or order our catalogue